Buckle Down®

3D Science

for the 21st Century

Elementary 5

Buckle Down 3-D Science for the 21st Century, Grade 5
B141NAW
ISBN-13: 978-1-63403-470-8

Cover Image: © Thinkstock

Contributing Editor: Christine Malik

Triumph Learning® New York, NY

Printed in the United States of America.

10 9 8 7 6 5 4 3 2 1

www.triumphlearning.com

What's 3-D about 3-D Science?

If you have seen a 3-D movie, you know that you need to wear special glasses. When you look through the glasses, objects in the movie appear solid, as they do in the real world. They have three dimensions—depth as well as length and width. You may feel as though you are right there in the movie.

You can think of science as having three dimensions, too. One dimension is made up of core ideas that explain the natural world. These ideas answer specific questions in physical sciences, life sciences, and Earth and space sciences. They make up the body of scientific knowledge.

A second dimension is made up of concepts that connect all the areas of science. Some of these concepts are patterns, systems, and cause and effect. For example, scientists find patterns in materials, in the motion of objects, in living things, and in Earth's features.

The third dimension is made up of scientific practices. These are the ways scientists think and learn about the natural world. Scientists ask questions, use models, and argue from evidence. They carry out investigations, analyze data, and communicate.

3-D Science for the 21st Century will help you put all the dimensions together. You won't just read about science. You will do science. You will look at the natural world as a scientist—no 3-D glasses required!

Disciplinary Core Ideas

Crosscutting Concepts

Science and Engineering Practices

Contents

Structure and Properties of Matter

What do a smartphone and a frog have in common?

In this unit, you are going to explore what scientists call matter. What is matter? What is matter made of? Can you always see it? How does it behave? Do all types of matter behave in the same way?

You will find that matter behaves in some predictable ways. And that knowledge will help you answer many questions about your world—about frogs and smartphones, and much more.

Lesson 1

What Makes Up Matter?

Look closely at the photos.

Each photo shows something found in nature. Discuss the photos with a partner. Try to identify the objects shown in the photos. How are the objects different from each other? Can you think of any ways in which they are alike? Record your ideas on the lines below.

Now look around your classroom, and choose three different objects. How are they different from the objects in the photos? Are there any ways in which all six objects are alike? Record your ideas.

One way to describe all six objects is to say that they take up space, or have volume. You cannot put one object in the same space as another object. They also have weight. If you put each object on a scale, it will show the object's weight in units such as grams or ounces.

Scientists have a word for anything that takes up space and has weight. They call it **matter**—the "stuff" that makes up the physical world.

Do you think that air is matter? Explain your answer.

Look Ahead

The world around us is made up of matter. But what makes up matter? How can it have so many different forms? These are questions that you will start to explore in this lesson.

Explore!

Disappearing Matter

Materials

- 150 milliliters of water
- Hand lens
- Set of measuring spoons
- 3 tablespoons of sugar
- 4 plastic spoons

Steps

1 Observe the water in your cup. When you observe something in science, you use your senses. Your five senses include sight, sound, touch, taste, and smell. Look at the water with your eyes alone and then with the hand lens. Describe what you see.

_____

_____

_____

2 Use a spoon to take a sip of water. Describe how the water feels in your mouth. Then describe its taste.

_____

_____

_____

Safety First!

Never taste a substance in a science lab unless your teacher tells you to.

3 Observe the sugar with your eyes alone and then with the hand lens. Describe what you see.

_____

_____

_____

4 Use a clean spoon to take a small taste of sugar. Describe how the sugar feels in your mouth. Then describe its taste.

_____

_____

_____

5 Add 2 teaspoons of sugar to the water. Stir with a clean spoon until the sugar disappears. Use the hand lens to observe the water. Describe what you see.

_____

_____

_____

6 Use a clean spoon to take a sip of water. Describe how it feels in your mouth. Then describe its taste.

_____

_____

_____

Think About It

Describe what you think happened to the sugar. Use what you observed to support your idea.

Share your findings and thoughts with the other members of your group, and listen to their ideas. Use the lines below if you want to revise your own idea about what happened to the sugar.

Understand

When you used a hand lens to observe water and sugar, you most likely saw more than when you used your eyes alone. You may have seen more bubbles in the water. You may have seen that the grains of sugar have many sides. But you did not see what makes up these kinds of matter.

All matter is made up of very tiny particles. The particles are much too small to be seen with a hand lens or with any other tool in your classroom.

One way to study the particles of matter is to use models. A model represents a real object, system, or process. Most often, a model is simpler than what it represents. It may also be larger or smaller than what it represents. Scientists use many different kinds of models. You will make and use some of them throughout this book.

Science Tools

Objects in nature range from the very large to the very small. Scientists use a variety of tools to help them see small objects. A hand lens is one tool that magnifies objects, or makes them appear larger. You can use a hand lens to observe the veins of a leaf or the grains of a rock. A microscope magnifies objects much more than a hand lens. For example, you can use a microscope to view the tiny parts called cells that make up a leaf.

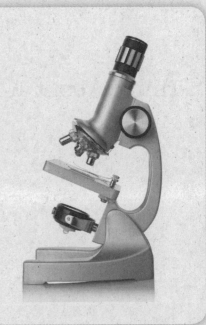

The kind of microscope you will use in school is shown here. It is called a compound light microscope. However, the particles of matter are so tiny that scientists must use other kinds of microscopes to view the particles.

A diagram is one kind of model. The diagrams below are models of a solid, a liquid, and a gas. The models show how the particles are arranged in those three states, or forms, of matter.

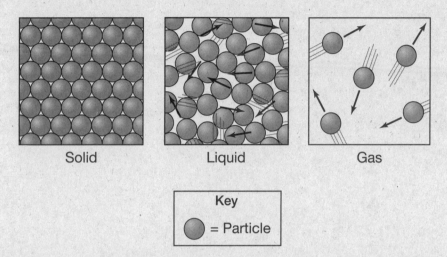

Solid   Liquid   Gas

Key

● = Particle

How does the size of the particles in the diagrams compare with the size of real particles of matter?

A solid is matter that has a fixed shape and a fixed volume. A solid keeps its shape unless something breaks or bends it. The amount of space it takes up does not change. The particles of a solid are packed tightly together. They vibrate, or move back and forth very fast, but they do not move away from their places. Ice is the solid form of water. Your desk and books and parts of your body are also solids.

A liquid is matter that has a fixed volume but not a fixed shape. It takes the shape of its container. The particles of a liquid are not as tightly packed as those of a solid. They can slide past each other. That is why the shape of a liquid can change. Liquid water is the most important liquid on Earth. Oils are also liquids.

A gas is matter that does not have a fixed shape or a fixed volume. A gas spreads out in all directions and fills its container. The particles of a gas are much farther apart than the particles of a solid or liquid. They move around easily and bounce off each other. The gas form of water, called water vapor, is one of the gases in our air.

In the models of a liquid and a gas, what do the arrows represent?

Many substances dissolve in liquid water. In other words, they break down into particles that mix evenly with the water particles and seem to disappear.

Turn back to the Explore activity. Reread the activity and your notes about your observations. Think about what you have learned about matter. Then, in the space below, draw a model that shows what happened to the sugar that you stirred into the water. Include a key like the one for the models on the previous page. Remember that you need to show two kinds of particles.

Exchange models with a partner, and discuss the models with each other. Does your partner understand your model? Use the space below to revise your model if you need to make it clearer or if you change your ideas.

Go Further

Scientists are like detectives. They observe and ask questions. They gather evidence and try to understand it. Then they draw conclusions. You followed those steps to solve the mystery of the disappearing sugar. But scientists do not stop there. They build their knowledge by using what they learn to try to answer new questions. The particle models in this lesson can help you answer more questions about matter.

Earth's air is made up of several different gases mixed together. Look back at the model of a gas. How does the model help explain why you cannot see the air around you?

Although you cannot see air, you can observe its effects. Look closely at the photo below.

What do you see that tells you what the air was doing when the photo was taken?

How can you use your senses of touch and hearing to observe air?

Gases are a form of matter. Since air is made up of gases, air must be matter, too. Remember that matter has weight and volume. It is hard to weigh air with the tools in your classroom, but you can test whether air has volume, or takes up space.

Try This

Blow air from your lungs into a balloon. When it is partly inflated but still soft, tie the open end, and squeeze the balloon in the middle. Describe what happens to the balloon, and use what you know about matter to explain why.

_____

_____

_____

_____

When a puddle dries up, the liquid water evaporates, or changes to a gas. It seems to disappear.

What happens to the water particles? You can use the models of a solid, a liquid, and a gas to help you answer this question.

Keep the particle models of matter in mind as you explore other topics in Units 1 and 2 of this book. They will help you understand how matter changes and how it moves between living things.

1   Select each sentence that describes **all** matter.

   A ☐ It can be seen.

   B ☐ It has volume.

   C ☐ It is solid or liquid.

   D ☐ It has weight.

   E ☐ It is made up of particles.

2   Which sentence **best** explains why a tire gets flat if air leaks out of it?

   A ☐ Air has weight.

   B ☐ Air cannot be seen.

   C ☐ Air takes up space.

   D ☐ Air spreads out in all directions.

3   Compare solids, liquids, and gases. For each form of matter, mark an X in the box next to each phrase that describes it.

	Solid	Liquid	Gas
Takes up space			
Has a fixed shape			
Has weight			
Has a fixed volume			

4   In the box below, draw a model showing how particles are arranged in a block of wood.

5   The model you made in question 4 is much larger than what it represents. Explain why that is useful.

_____

_____

_____

_____

Lesson 2

Observing Properties of Matter

Study the photo carefully.

Discuss the photo with a partner. Describe the objects in detail. In what ways are the objects alike? In what ways are they different? Record your ideas on the lines below.

How could the details that you listed help you identify one specific doll in the group? Explain your answer below.

Work with a partner. Think of an object that you would like to describe. Do not tell your partner what it is. Your partner must be able to identify the object based only on your description. Use the following questions as a guide.

What object have you chosen? Think about the object's size, color, shape, and texture, or how it feels. Also think about how the object is used. What do you think are the four most important features needed to identify the object?

Share these features with your partner. Have your partner record the features. Your partner will also choose an object. When it is your turn to guess, your partner will share four features needed to identify the object.

Study the information your partner gave you. In the space below, draw a picture of the object you have identified. Then compare your results with your partner's.

Look Ahead

In this lesson, you will learn about properties that help you tell one kind of matter from another.

Explore!

What Difference Can a Property of Matter Make?

Materials

- 2 Styrofoam cups
- 1 metal spoon
- 1 plastic spoon
- Water
- Thermometer
- Timer or clock

Steps

1 Set the cups and spoons on a table. Your teacher will pour hot water into each cup. Use the thermometer to measure the temperature of the water in each cup. Leave the thermometer in each cup for at least 2 or 3 minutes before noting the temperature. Record the temperature of the water in each cup below.

Safety First!

Use caution when handling any hot materials or objects.

_____

_____

2 Touch each of the spoons on the table. Does either spoon feel warm to the touch? Does either spoon feel cold to the touch?

_____

_____

3 Place one spoon in each cup. Set a timer to ring in 3 minutes, or use a clock to measure the 3 minutes. Then touch both spoons again. Record your observations on the lines below.

Plastic spoon    Metal spoon

_____

_____

Think About It

Compare how the two spoons felt. What was the difference between the spoons? What was the difference between the cups of water?

What can you conclude about the properties of a metal spoon and a plastic spoon?

Suppose you want to make a pot handle that will not get hot when the pot is heated. Which material will you choose, metal or plastic? Explain your choice.

Understand

In Lesson 1, you learned that everything is made up of matter. Matter is anything that has weight and takes up space. A block of wood and a cube of sugar are types of matter. So are a drop of water and the helium gas in a balloon.

All matter has properties that you can observe with your senses or measure with tools. Color, texture, and taste are some properties of matter. Different types of matter have different properties. A type of matter is called a substance or a material.

In the activity at the beginning of this lesson, the features that you listed about the object are its properties. A property is a physical characteristic of an object or material. A property can be the way something looks or feels.

Some properties describe how well a material can do something. In the Explore activity, you observed how well two materials conduct heat. A good conductor lets heat pass through easily. The metal spoon got warmer than the plastic spoon because metal conducts heat well. Some materials that do not conduct heat well are cloth, plastic, and rubber.

Look carefully at the photo above. Why would a person use a spoon made of wood?

There are many other properties of matter. Some materials reflect light better than others. Look at the photos above. The pan in the photo on the left is made of stainless steel. The pan on the right is made of iron.

Which pan do you think reflects more light? Describe how that pan is different from the other pan.

Science Tools

In the Explore activity, you used your sense of touch to observe how well plastic and metal conduct heat. There is another way to tell how well a material conducts heat. You can use a thermometer to measure the temperature of a material before and after it has been heated.

Temperature is a measure of how warm or cold something is. A thermometer may show temperature in degrees Celsius (°C) or degrees Fahrenheit (°F). Many thermometers show both temperature scales. Look at the thermometer to the right. It shows a temperature of 20°C, which is equal to 68°F. Scientists usually measure temperature in degrees Celsius.

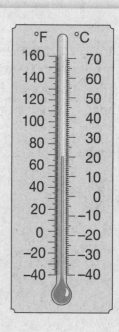

You can observe whether a magnet attracts a material. A magnet attracts some metals. These include iron, nickel, and cobalt. Steel is made with iron. So a magnet attracts paper clips, staples, and food cans made of steel. A magnet does not attract other metals, such as copper and aluminum. And a magnet does not attract nonmetals, such as glass, plastic, wood, or rubber.

How could you use the property described above to sort a mixed pile of plastic paper clips and steel paper clips? Explain your answer.

You can also observe whether a material dissolves in water. Think back to the Explore activity in Lesson 1. You observed that sugar dissolves in water. Recall that when a substance dissolves, it breaks down into tiny particles that seem to disappear. Some substances dissolve in water, and some do not.

What do you think would happen if you put sand into a cup of warm water and stirred it? Give an example in nature that supports your answer.

You can observe whether a material conducts electricity. Electricity moves easily through some materials but not through others. Many substances that conduct heat well also conduct electricity. Metals such as copper and iron are good conductors of electricity. Most nonmetals are not good conductors of electricity. The diagrams below show two electric circuits.

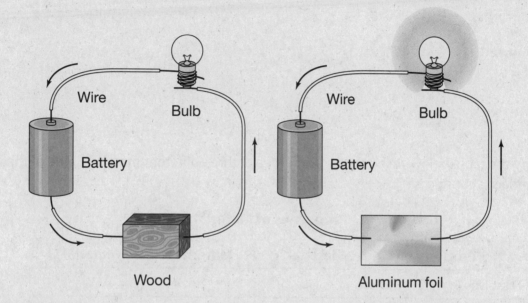

Think back to the Explore activity and what you have learned about materials that conduct heat or electricity. Then compare the diagrams. Why is one bulb lit and the other is not?

Go Further

Scientists study the properties of a material to identify it. But more than one property is usually needed to identify a material.

Explain why you think scientists must observe several properties to identify a material. Give an example.

Study the table below. It shows the properties of three different materials. One of the materials is copper.

Properties of Materials

Property	Material A	Material B	Material C
Dissolves in water	No	No	Yes
Conducts electricity	Yes	Yes	No
Is attracted to a magnet	Yes	No	No
Reflects light well	No	Yes	No

Which of these materials can you identify as copper? Explain why.

Try This

Observe objects in your classroom to find five that are reflective. Then use a magnet to test whether the objects are also magnetic. Record your findings in the table below.

Reflective Object	Is It Magnetic?

Which of the two properties is more useful for identifying a material? Explain.

_____

_____

_____

1 Which sentence **best** describes a material that is a good conductor?

A ⭘ It is attracted by a magnet.

B ⭘ It can be dissolved in water.

C ⭘ Heat and electricity move easily through it.

D ⭘ Electricity cannot move through it.

2 Select all the objects that a magnet will attract.

A ⭘ an aluminum can

B ⭘ a drinking glass

C ⭘ an iron tool

D ⭘ a wooden birdhouse

E ⭘ a staple made of steel

F ⭘ a rubber glove

3 Compare the properties of sugar, wood, and iron. For each material, mark an X to show each property that describes it.

Property	Sugar	Wood	Iron
Dissolves in water			
Conducts heat			
Conducts electricity			
Is attracted to a magnet			
Reflects light well			

4 Select all the properties that describe copper.

    A ◯ It conducts heat.

    B ◯ It is reflective.

    C ◯ It is magnetic.

    D ◯ It dissolves in water.

    E ◯ It conducts electricity.

5 A scientist wants to investigate the identity of an unknown substance. The scientist thinks that the unknown substance is made up of particles of aluminum. What properties could the scientist test for? Describe the properties.

_____

_____

_____

_____

How Matter Changes

Observe each photo carefully.

Discuss the photos with a partner. What is happening in each photo?

Which of these photos shows what happened first? Why do you think so? What changes have taken place between the time that the first photo was taken and the second photo was taken?

Matter can change when substances mix together. A substance can be a solid, a liquid, or a gas. You saw an example of this in the photos of the burning wood and the ash. When wood burns, oxygen in the air mixes with the wood. When they mix, ash and other materials, such as gases, are produced.

Look at the photo above. The iron in the steel body of the old truck mixed with oxygen in the air to form a different material. The material that formed is rust.

What are some ways you see matter changing in your own environment?

Look Ahead

Matter changes are all around. Does matter always change when things mix together? In this lesson, you will investigate how matter changes.

How Matter Changes

Materials

- 75 milliliters of whole milk
- 75 milliliters of red vinegar
- 2 clear glass jars with screw-top lids
- Tablespoon
- Craft stick

- Clear plastic cup
- Basket-style coffee filter
- Rubber band
- Paper towels

Steps

1 Your teacher will give you a jar containing 75 milliliters of milk and another jar containing 75 milliliters of vinegar. Observe the jar of milk. Gently swirl the jar of milk. What properties, or physical characteristics, of the milk do you observe? Record your observations on the lines below.

_____

_____

_____

Safety First! Never taste anything in science class unless your teacher tells you to.

2 Next, observe the jar of vinegar. Gently swirl the jar to observe the liquid. What properties, or physical characteristics, of the vinegar do you observe? Record your observations below.

_____

_____

_____

3 Carefully open each jar. Add 1 tablespoon of vinegar to the milk. Use a craft stick to gently stir the milk and vinegar. Observe and record what happens.

_____

_____

_____

4 Next, carefully pour the rest of the vinegar into the milk jar. Gently swirl. Let the mixture settle for about 5 minutes. Observe and record what happens.

_____

_____

5 Use the rubber band to fasten the coffee filter over the clear plastic cup. Gently push the middle of the filter down into the cup. Carefully pour the mixture through the coffee filter and into the cup. This may take 20–30 minutes. When most of the liquid has passed through the filter, observe what is in the coffee filter. Record your observations below.

_____

_____

_____

_____

Think About It

What do you think happened to the milk and the vinegar? Do you think the substance in the filter could be separated back into milk and vinegar?

Share your findings and thoughts with the other members of your group, and listen to their ideas. Use the lines below if you want to revise your own ideas.

Understand

Sometimes when you mix things together, the things you mix stay the same as they were before you mixed them—nothing changes. For example, you observed that a different substance did not form when sugar was dissolved in water in Lesson 1.

Look at the photo of the fruit salad on the right.

What happens when you mix slices of banana and kiwifruit to make a fruit salad? Does matter change in this mixture? Record your ideas on the lines below.

Sometimes matter changes when you mix things together. A different kind of matter forms. When some substances are mixed, they react with each other. They combine in ways to form other substances. Old matter is not lost. It just changes to a different kind of matter. The kind of matter it changes to has different properties than the substances that were mixed together to form it. When a different kind of matter forms, the change is more than just purely physical.

Many changes that are purely physical can be reversed. Look at the photo of the tray of ice cubes.

If the tray of ice cubes is left out on a kitchen counter, what will happen? If there is a change, can the change be reversed? Will a different kind of matter form?

How can you tell whether a change is purely physical or that a different substance has formed? You can ask whether the change can be easily reversed. When a different substance is formed, it is much harder to reverse. In fact, some changes cannot be reversed at all. When you mix vinegar with baking soda, the mixture gives off a gas. The gas that forms cannot change back into the original two substances.

Think back to the photos of the wood burning and the ash left behind. Can that change be reversed? Explain your answer below.

Some mixtures give signs, or clues, that a different kind of matter has formed. You can observe mixtures for these signs. With some mixtures, there might be a temperature change, which you can measure. Color changes can happen, too. Sometimes light is given off. You can observe light and color with your own eyes. Look at the photo below. When you bend the glow stick, it lights up.

The light from a glow stick is a sign that a different kind of matter has formed. How do you think that happens? Record your ideas.

The table below lists some signs that tell you a different kind of matter may have formed. However, these are only signs that something has changed. Sometimes when some of these signs appear, a different kind of matter has not formed. For example, the bubbles that form in boiling water do not mean that a different kind of matter has formed.

Signs That a Different Kind of Matter May Have Formed

Sign	Examples
A substance changes color.	An apple core turns brown. Egg white changes from clear to white.
A substance has a different odor.	Burning wood smells different from freshly cut wood. Spoiled food smells bad.
A substance changes temperature without being heated or cooled.	Rotting leaves in a compost pile become warm. Vinegar becomes cooler when it is mixed with baking soda.
Bubbles form in a substance.	Bubbles form when vinegar is mixed with baking soda. Bubbles form in pancake batter as the pancakes cook.
A substance gives off a gas or gases.	Burning wood gives off carbon dioxide and water vapor. A mixture of vinegar and baking soda gives off carbon dioxide.
A different kind of solid forms.	Rust forms on an iron nail. Tarnish forms on a silver spoon.

What sign of a change in matter was present in the Explore activity? What did that change tell you? Was a different kind of matter formed? Record your ideas.

How do you know that a different kind of matter does not form when you mix banana and kiwifruit slices to make a fruit salad?

Go Further

Raising the temperature can also cause materials to change. Materials mixed together, like the ingredients to make a cake, change when they are heated. When you bake cake batter or cook a raw egg, you raise the temperature. This causes a different kind of matter to form. After some time, the changes stop happening. But the baked cake has different properties from the batter. The cake is a different kind of matter.

What are the signs that a different kind of matter has formed when a cake is baked?

Look at the photo above of a candle being lit. As the candle burns, what signs will there be that a different kind of matter is being formed?

Look at the photo above of an antacid tablet that has been dropped into a glass of water. Do you think a different kind of matter, or a different substance, is forming? Explain.

Think about the antacid tablet being dropped into the glass of water. Do you think the temperature of the water would affect the results? Design an experiment in which you can investigate this question. Write a list of materials below. Then describe the steps of your procedure. Write a question that you would like to answer in your investigation.

Materials

Procedure

Question

Check Your Understanding

1 Which of these is **most likely** to happen when oxygen mixes with iron?

A ◯ bubbling

B ◯ burning

C ◯ rotting

D ◯ rusting

2 Which of the following statements are signs that let you know a different kind of matter may have formed? Select all that apply.

A ◯ A substance melts.

B ◯ A substance gives off gas.

C ◯ A substance breaks apart.

D ◯ A substance gives off an odor.

E ◯ A substances releases bubbles.

F ◯ A substance forms rust or tarnish.

3 Look at the picture below.

Apple core ⟶ Rotting apple core

Which of these **most likely** caused the change you see in the picture?

A ◯ Fire burned the apple.

B ◯ Oxygen mixed with the apple.

C ◯ Vinegar mixed with the apple.

D ◯ Heat was applied to the apple.

4   Which of these is an example of a different kind of matter, or a different substance, forming as a result of a change?

  A ☐ Bubbles have formed in boiling soup.

  B ☐ A wax crayon has melted in the sun.

  C ☐ A banana has turned brown.

  D ☐ A juice box has frozen.

5   Look at each picture. Mark the box with an X to tell whether it is a change that is purely physical or one in which a different substance formed.

	Change Is Purely Physical	Different Substance Formed
Sugar cube ⟶ Sugar granules		
Log ⟶ Ash		
Batter ⟶ Cake		
Ice ⟶ Liquid water		

How Matter Stays the Same

Study each photo carefully.

Discuss the photos with a partner. Describe what is happening. Record your answer on the lines below.

What kind of matter do you see in each photo? How is the matter in each photo changing its properties? Where does the matter in each photo go after it changes?

Study the photo on the right.

What will happen to the ice and the water in the glass if the glass sits on a sunny windowsill for two hours?

What will happen to the temperature of the water in the glass if the glass continues to sit on the sunny windowsill for two more hours?

Look Ahead

Changes in matter happen all the time. In this lesson, you will investigate what happens to matter when it changes form.

Explore!

Can Matter Be Lost?

Materials

- 4 ice cubes
- Plastic cup
- Plastic wrap
- Double pan balance
- Standard gram weights

Steps

1 Place the ice cubes in the plastic cup. Cover the cup with the plastic wrap. Place the covered cup of ice cubes in one pan of the balance.

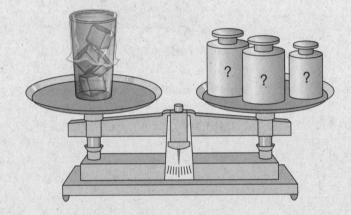

2 Measure the gram weight of the covered cup of ice cubes by adding weights to the other pan until the pans balance. Record your measurement below.

_____

3 Place the covered cup of ice cubes in a warm or sunny place for several hours.

4 After several hours have passed, weigh the covered cup and melted ice on the pan balance. Record your measurement below. What happened to the ice?

_____

_____

5 Place the covered cup in the freezer overnight. Then weigh the cup on the pan balance again. Record your measurement below. What happened to the water?

_____

_____

_____

6 In the space below, draw a bar graph to show the three measurements you took. Label the bottom axis _before melting_, _liquid water_, and _after freezing_. Show a scale of your gram measurements along the other axis.

_____

_____

_____

Think About It

Compare the measurements that you took. What can you conclude about the changes in matter that you observed?

Understand

Matter is able to change form. Liquid water evaporates into water vapor. Sugar dissolves into a cup of liquid. Matter may seem to disappear, but it is still there. It is just in a different form.

In the Explore activity, you let ice cubes melt into liquid water. Then you refroze the water so that it changed back into ice. What happened? Even though the water changed from solid to liquid and back again, the amount of water stayed the same. Scientists have a word to describe that when matter changes, the amount of matter always stays the same. The word is *conserved*. When matter is conserved, none of it is lost. Look at the photo of the iceberg. When an iceberg melts, the water goes into the ocean. The water will not disappear. It will be conserved.

How do you know that water was conserved during the Explore activity?

Describe another example in nature that shows how matter can be conserved.

Many other substances undergo similar changes. For example, a metal can melt into liquid when it is heated. It changes back to a solid when it cools and hardens. Many industries apply this property of metals in the real world. The photo above on the left shows molten, or liquid, metal being poured into a mold. Iron and a mixture of other substances are melted in a furnace. The molten mixture is poured into a mold. When the mixture cools, it forms a molded piece of a metal called steel.

How did matter shown in each photo change?

How could you prove that the same amount of matter was present before and after the change?

What sign of a change was present in the Explore activity? How is this similar to molten iron and solid steel?

Precious metals like gold can be melted or heated for shaping into rings, earrings, necklaces, and other items. Look at the photo of gold earrings on the right.

Why would it be important for a jewelry maker to know that matter is conserved even when it changes?

A mixture of sand, gravel, and a substance called pitch is used to make asphalt. Asphalt is used to surface roads. The mixture is heated and poured onto a prepared roadbed. Then the asphalt is flattened by a steamroller. As it cools, the asphalt hardens into a strong, smooth surface for vehicles to travel on. Look at the photo on the right.

How does the conservation of matter apply to preparing the materials needed for surfacing a road?

Matter can be conserved even if it seems to vanish. Look at the photo of the ocean on the left above. Salt is dissolved in ocean water. You cannot see the dissolved salt in ocean water, just as you could not see the sugar you dissolved in water in Lesson 1.

Sometimes people remove the salt from salt water. They allow the water to evaporate, like water evaporates from a puddle on a hot day. The photo on the right above shows a salt evaporation pond. The piles look like snow, but they are made of salt. Water from an ocean or a salty sea is fed into large ponds. The water evaporates, leaving the salt behind. People then gather up the salt.

If you mix salt into water, how could you prove that the salt did not disappear, without tasting the water?

Some substances change properties when mixed. In Lesson 3, you read about how burning wood left a pile of ash behind. Even if the properties of the substances change, the total amount of the matter is conserved.

What do you think happened to the rest of the matter after the wood burned?

Go Further

In Lesson 3, you mixed liquids together to see how they acted. Solids, like salt and pepper, can also be mixed together. But mixing solids does not change the total amount of the substances. The diagram below shows a pile of sand grains and a pile of iron filings. Think about what happens when the two piles are mixed together. Study the labels.

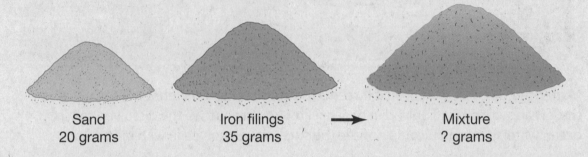

Sand
20 grams

Iron filings
35 grams

Mixture
? grams

How can you find out whether matter is conserved after the sand and iron filings are mixed?

Now study the diagram below.

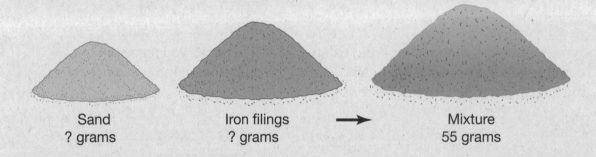

Sand
? grams

Iron filings
? grams

Mixture
55 grams

How can you find out whether matter was conserved if the sand and iron filings have already been mixed?

Matter is conserved when you mix substances together. But matter is also conserved when you separate it, or take it apart. You found that you can use a magnet to separate a mixture of iron filings and sand. The total amount of the sand and iron filings will be conserved when they are mixed together and when they are separated again. Matter can also be separated, or taken apart, by cutting it into pieces, like the apple you see in the photo. Matter can even be crushed or ground into powder and still be conserved.

How could you confirm that matter is conserved?

Try This

- Place 5 sugar cubes in a cup.
- Weigh the sugar cubes and cup on a pan balance. Record the weight.
- Remove the cup from the balance. Use a metal spoon to crush the sugar.
- Weigh the sugar and cup again. Record the results.

Before: Sugar cubes	After: Crushed sugar

Analyze the amounts of matter before and after crushing the cubes. Does changing the shape change the amount of matter? Explain.

_____

_____

1 Look at the picture below.

Before 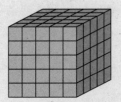   After

Select all the ways that you could find out that matter has been conserved.

A ◯ Take apart all the cubes without counting them.

B ◯ Count the cubes before and after.

C ◯ Weigh the cubes before and after.

D ◯ Add more cubes after you count them.

E ◯ Take away cubes after you count them.

2 A student records the following data in a table.

Weights of Ice and Water

Trial Number	Before	After Heating	After Cooling
1	28 grams	?	28 grams
2	?	37 grams	37 grams
3	15 grams	15 grams	?

Which would **most likely** be the missing weight for trial number 3?

A ◯ 15 grams

B ◯ 22 grams

C ◯ 30 grams

D ◯ 65 grams

3 Which statement **best** describes how matter can be conserved?

A ◯ The state of the matter does not change.

B ◯ The amount of matter does not change.

C ◯ The properties of matter do not change.

D ◯ The form of the matter does not change.

4 Look at the picture below. What is the weight of the tongue depressors made into a cube? Explain how you know.

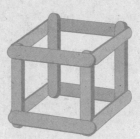

12 tongue depressors
in a stack

12 tongue depressors
built to make a cube

16.5 grams

? grams

_____

_____

5 Which of the following statements about the sugar granules shown below is **not** correct?

Sugar cube ⟶ Sugar granules

A ◯ They weigh more than the sugar cube.

B ◯ They weigh the same as the sugar cube.

C ◯ The matter in the sugar granules has been conserved.

D ◯ The matter in the cube and granules have the same properties.

Lesson 5

Why Matter Stays on Earth

Look carefully at each photo above.

Discuss the photos with a partner. Record your observations about what you see in the photos on the lines below.

Where will the rocks go if they fall from the side of the cliff? Where does the water go as it flows over the rocks?

Study the objects in the photos below.

Discuss the objects in the photos with a partner. Then describe the objects on the lines below. What might happen if you dropped each object?

Why do objects like those you observed in the photos on these pages seem to drop by themselves?

Look Ahead

A force is a push or a pull. In this lesson, you will investigate different forces that act on objects on Earth.

Explore!

Forces at Work

Materials

- Crayon
- Coin
- Paper clip
- Marker
- Foam ball

Steps

1 Pick two objects. Hold them straight out in front of you at the same distance from the floor. Then drop them at the same time. In the table below, record your observations about how the objects fall. Do this three times, or in three trials, each time with the same two objects.

	Trial 1	Trial 2	Trial 3
Objects _____ _____ _____			
Observations _____ _____ _____ _____			

2 Gently toss the foam ball, underhand, to a partner. Then catch the ball when your partner tosses it back.

3 Observe as two other partners toss and catch the ball. Record your observations. Draw a diagram of the path of the ball.

_____

_____

Think About It

Compare the motion of the dropped objects and the tossed ball. What was the same? What was different?

Share your diagram and observations of the path of the ball with your group. Based on the diagrams and your observations, did the ball follow approximately the same path each time it was thrown? Explain.

Understand

Look at the photo of Earth below. The photo was taken from a satellite in space. You can see that Earth is shaped like a sphere, or a round ball. In this photo of Earth, the view is of part of the Western Hemisphere, which includes the continents of North America and South America. The word *hemisphere* means "half of a sphere." If you live in the United States, then you live on the continent of North America in the Western Hemisphere. If you study the photo carefully, you can see the shapes of the continents.

Earth is like a giant round ball in space. On the surface of that giant round ball are continents, oceans, houses, schools, and people. Did you ever wonder how people and objects keep from falling off of Earth? The answer is that the force of gravity pulls everything down toward the center of Earth. Gravity keeps you and everything on Earth from flying off into space.

There is a cause and effect relationship between gravity and all objects on Earth. Look again at the photos at the beginning of the lesson. Gravity caused the rocks and the water to fall. Their falling was the effect. You also observed this relationship in the Explore activity. Gravity was the cause and the downward fall of the objects was the effect.

An object's weight is a measure of the pull of gravity on the object. When you step on a bathroom scale, the scale measures the pull of Earth's gravity on your body. What if a friend stepped onto a bathroom scale with you? The force measured by the scale would increase. This is because the scale is now measuring the pull of gravity on two people instead of one person. The pull of gravity on your body and your friend's body will be the same whether you are at home, at school, or anywhere else on Earth.

Science Tools: Spring Scale

Weight is a measure of the pull of gravity on an object. A spring scale is a tool that measures this pull of gravity. By attaching an object to the hook on the bottom of the scale and holding the scale vertically, you can measure the object's weight. A spring scale can also be used to measure other forces, such as the amount of force needed to pull an object.

The southernmost point on Earth is the geographic South Pole. It is located on the continent of Antarctica. Look again at the satellite photo of Earth. Place your finger at the very bottom of Earth's image. This is the location of the continent of Antarctica. The photo below shows a ship sailing in the ocean around Antarctica.

What keeps the ocean water around Antarctica from flowing out into space?

Explain how the ship sailing on the ocean at the very bottom of Earth's sphere is evidence of the force of gravity.

Below is another satellite image of Earth. Observe the photo carefully.

In this photo, the land seen on the lower right is the continent of Australia. Australia is in the Eastern Hemisphere of Earth. It is on the other side of the world from North America.

Think about the Explore activity you performed. If students in a classroom in Australia performed the same activity, what would happen to the objects they dropped?

Do all objects fall down toward the center of Earth, even when they are dropped from opposite sides of Earth? Explain.

Your results in the Explore activity are evidence of the force of gravity and how it works. Gravity has a cause and effect relationship on all the objects on Earth. Objects fall to the ground when they are dropped because the force of gravity pulls everything down toward the center of Earth. The force of gravity acts on objects in the same way all over the world.

You cannot see gravity, but you can see its effect on the motion of objects. When you let go of an object in the Explore activity, it fell down to the floor. When you tossed the ball to your partner, did your partner always catch it? What happens if you toss a ball in the air and no one catches it? The ball does not keep sailing through the air. Gravity pulls the ball down until it hits the ground. Gravity also changes the direction of motion of an object moving through the air. When you hit a ball upward and outward, gravity pulls it down in a curved path. Look at the diagram below of a girl hitting a baseball.

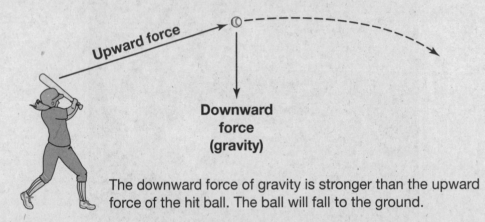

The downward force of gravity is stronger than the upward force of the hit ball. The ball will fall to the ground.

In the space below, draw your own diagram of a baseball after it has been hit by a batter. Use arrows to show the forces acting on the ball.

Gravity acts by pulling objects down toward Earth's center. What evidence of this is shown in your drawing? Explain.

Go Further

Earth's gravity pulls everything on Earth down toward Earth's center. Sports such as sledding, skiing, and snowboarding depend on gravity moving people and objects down a slope. Gravity is always acting on objects on Earth. Gravity pulls you even if you are not touching the ground. Look at the photo below of people skydiving.

Study the photo of the skydivers above. Use the space below to draw a picture of a person skydiving. Add arrows to your picture to show how gravity is acting on the skydiver.

What might happen if the force of gravity did not pull the skydiver toward Earth?

Materials

- Metric ruler
- 1-meter length of string
- Pencil

Tie the pencil onto one end of the string. Now tie the other end of the string onto one end of the ruler. Be sure it is tied on tightly so that it cannot fall off. You can use tape to hold it more securely, if needed.

Hold the ruler straight out, with each end the same distance from the floor. The pencil on the string should be hanging straight down toward the floor. Now slowly begin to lift, or tilt, one end of the ruler up until the ruler is pointing straight up in the air. As you are tilting the ruler, observe how the pencil on the string moves.

Now do the reverse. Slowly lift, or tilt, the ruler so that the other end of the ruler is straight up in the air. Again, observe how the pencil moves.

What evidence of the force of gravity did you observe when you tilted the ruler one way and then the other?

1 Look at the picture of a boy kicking a soccer ball.

Draw an arrow to show the path of the ball after the boy kicks it. Label the direction of gravity.

_____

_____

_____

2 Which of these causes an object on Earth to have weight?

A ◯ the force of gravity

B ◯ the spherical shape of Earth

C ◯ the way it falls straight downward

D ◯ the path of its motion through the air

3 Which action is the **best** example of the cause and effect relationship between gravity and all objects on Earth?

A ◯ A ball rolls along a floor.

B ◯ A toy car rolls to a stop.

C ◯ A bird flies through the air.

D ◯ A rock falls toward Earth.

4 Look at the picture below. How is the motion of the basketball evidence of the force of gravity on Earth?

_____

_____

_____

5 Which of the following statements about the way the force of gravity acts is correct? Select all that apply.

A ◯ Dropped objects fall straight down to the ground.

B ◯ Objects that are held and dropped fall in a curved path.

C ◯ Gravity changes the direction of an object that is thrown.

D ◯ People all over Earth observe that objects fall straight down.

E ◯ Only objects that are dropped, and not thrown, fall to Earth's surface.

Matter and Energy in Living Things

What did you have for dinner last night? In this unit, you will learn how the sun, the soil, the air, other animals, and even bacteria helped provide that dinner.

How do plants obtain food? How do animals get energy from plants or from other animals? How are the sun, the air, water, and soil involved in these processes? These are some questions you will consider in this lesson.

You will learn why living things need matter as well as energy. By the end of the unit, you will be able to answer this question: How is eating your dinner like recycling?

Lesson 6

Energy for All Living Things

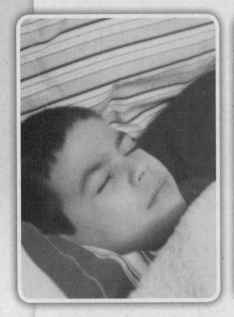  

Look closely at the photos.

Discuss the photos with a partner. What do the photos show? How might the activities in the photos be related? Record your ideas on the lines below.

Now look at the middle photo. What are the children doing? How are they using energy? How do the children get the energy to play? Record your ideas.

Every minute of the day, your body is using energy. Energy is the ability to make things move or change. Your body uses energy to move muscles when you breathe in and out. It uses energy when you blink your eyes. It uses energy when you run, jump, and play. It uses energy when you think. It even uses energy when you sleep!

Work with a partner. List at least ten ways the children in the photo are using energy. Record your ideas below.

Look Ahead

People are not the only living things that need energy. Every living thing needs energy to survive. How do living things get energy? In this lesson, you will investigate this question.

Explore!

Energy from Food

Materials

- Paper plates
- Markers
- 4" x 6" index cards
- Scissors
- Tape

Steps

1 Think about the foods you eat at different meals. With your group, choose a meal for which you can plan a menu. Record the meal you chose, and list some foods that you like to eat for that meal.

_____

_____

_____

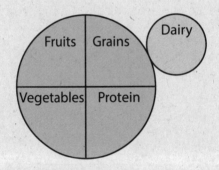

2 Use a marker to divide a paper plate into four equal sections. Label each section as shown. Cut out a large circle from an index card and label it _Dairy_. Tape the Dairy circle to the upper right section of your plate. Work with your group to brainstorm a list of foods in each group that could make up your meal. List your ideas below.

Safety First!
Use caution when using scissors.

_____

_____

_____

_____

3 Choose a food from each food group for your meal. Draw each food in the correct section of the plate or in the circle for dairy. Analyze your choices. Which foods come from plants? Which come from animals? Label each food with *Plant* or *Animal* to tell its source. Summarize your meal in the table below.

Food Group	Food I Chose	From Plant or Animal?
Fruits		
Grains		
Vegetables		
Protein		
Dairy		

4 Share your plate with other group members. Discuss the source of each food. Record all the foods chosen and whether they come from plants or animals.

_____

_____

_____

_____

Think About It

How do you get the energy you need to move, learn, and grow?

All living things need energy. The plants and animals you eat at a meal need to get energy, too. Where might animals get the energy they need? Where might plants get the energy they need? Write your ideas below.

Understand

When you worked with your group to develop a meal, you discovered that the foods we eat come from other living things. People, like other animals, need energy to move. Humans, other mammals, and birds use energy to stay warm. We get energy from food. The energy allows us to move, learn, and grow.

Another word for living things is *organisms*. Different kinds of organisms get energy in different ways. Plants use the energy of sunlight to make food. Plant leaves take in sunlight. Structures in the leaves use materials from air and water to make sugar. The sugar is the plants' food. Plants store leftover sugar in their leaves, stems, flowers, seeds, and roots. Because plants make their own food, they are called producers.

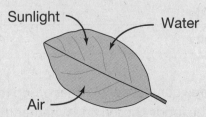

Animals cannot make their own food. They get energy by eating other living things. Organisms that eat other living things are called consumers. Some consumers eat mainly plants. When an animal eats a plant, energy from the sun passes from the plant to the animal. Only some energy in the plant is available to the animal. The plant uses most of its energy to grow.

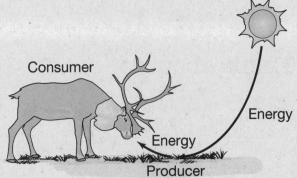

The photo and diagram show how a moose gets energy. Compare the photo and diagram. What does the diagram show that the photo does not?

Other consumers are meat eaters. They eat mainly other animals. When a meat eater eats another animal, it gets whatever energy the first animal had stored in its body. Some consumers, such as black bears and raccoons, eat both plants and other animals.

How does the salmon provide energy to the bear? Where did the salmon get its energy?

Reread the activity and your notes about the meal you planned. Think about what you have learned about where the energy your body needs comes from. Then, in the space below, write a paragraph explaining how a person gets energy. Give two examples of what a person can do with that energy.

Go Further

Energy from the sun passes from producers to the consumers that eat them. Each living thing stores only part of the energy from the plants or animals it eats. Each animal uses most of the energy it gets to keep warm, move around, and do many other things.

Food chains are models used to show how energy moves from one living thing to another. The arrows show the direction in which energy moves through the chain.

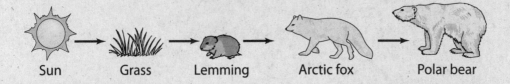

Sun → Grass → Lemming → Arctic fox → Polar bear

Look at the model of a food chain. What is the original source of energy in this food chain? How do you know?

Which organism in the chain is a producer? How do you know?

Which organisms in the chain are consumers? How do you know?

Remember that plants produce their own food, but animals do not. Animals need to eat plants or other animals in order to get energy.

Try This

Think of an animal that lives in your area. Make a food chain that includes that animal. You can draw and label the organisms you include or just use labels. Show how the animal gets energy and how it gives energy to another living thing. Make sure you include the original source of energy in your food chain.

Exchange food chain models with a partner. Discuss your food chains with each other. Did you each include the original source of energy for your chain? Do you have producers and consumers in your chain? Use the box below to revise your model food chain if you need to.

1 What is the original source of the energy people get from food?

A ○ plants

B ○ plant eaters

C ○ meat eaters

D ○ the sun

2 Compare the living things listed below. For each organism, mark an X in the box that tells whether it gets energy directly from the sun or from other living things.

Organism	Gets Energy Directly from the Sun	Gets Energy from Eating Other Living Things
Sunflower		
Tiger		
Squirrel		
Human		
Antelope		
Tree		

3 What do plants use to make their own food? Select each correct answer.

A ○ air

B ○ soil

C ○ sunlight

D ○ water

E ○ sugar

4   Make a food chain using four of the items in the box. Use arrows to show the
    direction in which energy moves.

| Caterpillar Cricket Fox Plant Hawk Rabbit Robin Snake Sun |

Lesson 7

Materials for Growth and Repair

Look closely at the photos.

Discuss these photos with a partner. What is shown in the photo on the left? How is it different from what is shown in the photo on the right? How is it the same? Try to identify specific similarities and differences. Record your ideas below.

What do you think a plant needs in order to grow? How does a plant get the materials it needs? Record your ideas.

Plants and animals are living things. All living things need materials to grow. There are many similarities and differences among living things and how they grow.

Look at the photo of a mother duck and her young ducklings. Ducklings like those shown in this photo will grow into mature adult ducks in about a year.

A tree seedling takes many years to grow into a mature tree. The seedling in the photo you observed is about 15 centimeters tall. The seedling can grow into a mature tree that is more than 21 meters tall.

What do animals need in order to grow? Where do the materials for growth come from? Discuss these ideas with a partner. Record your ideas below.

Look Ahead

All living things use materials to grow and to repair themselves when injured. Where do living things get the materials they need for growth? In this lesson, you will explore this question.

Explore!

Soil or Air?

Steps

1 Study the tomato plant in the photo above on the left. Describe the tomato plant, giving specific details about its features. Record your description below.

_____

_____

_____

2 Study the air plant in the photo above on the right. Notice that the air plant is sitting on the branch of another plant. Describe the air plant, giving specific details about its features. Record your description below.

_____

_____

_____

3 Use your descriptions of the tomato plant and the air plant to find ways in which the two plants are different and ways in which they are the same. Use what you find to fill in the Venn diagram below.

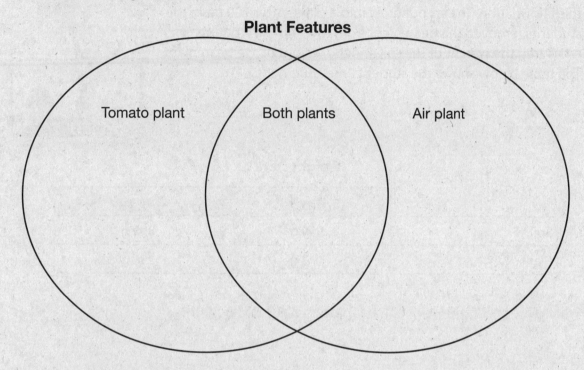

Plant Features

Tomato plant   Both plants   Air plant

Think About It

Think about your observations of the tomato plant. How do you think the tomato plant gets the materials it needs to live and grow?

Think about your observations of the air plant. How do you think the air plant gets the materials it needs to live and grow?

Understand

Some students measured the weight, in grams, of some soil and placed it in a container. Then they found the weight, in grams, of a bean seed sprout and planted the sprout in the soil. They recorded this information. The sprout grew into a plant. After 100 days, the students removed the bean plant from the soil. The students measured the weight of the soil and the weight of the bean plant. The table below shows the students' measurements.

Weight Data

	Day 1	Day 100
Soil	900 g	899 g
Plant	2 g	56 g

What is the change in weight of the soil from day 1 to day 100?

What is the change in weight of the plant from day 1 to day 100?

Compare the changes in weight of the soil and the plant. Which had the greater change in weight—the soil or the plant? Explain.

Can soil be the most important material used to make the new matter in the plant? Use evidence to support your argument.

Plants require certain materials in order to grow. Plants take in air and water. Recall that plants use air and water to make their own food. The food is a source of energy for the plants, but that is not all. The food also provides the materials that plants need for growth.

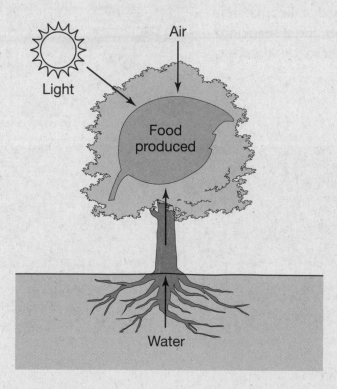

Study the diagram above. Compare this plant with the air plant that you observed in the Explore activity. Record your comparisons below.

Share your findings and thoughts with other members of the group, and listen to their ideas. Review your ideas about how the air plant you observed in the Explore activity gets the materials it needs to live and grow. Use the space below if you want to revise your ideas.

All animals, including humans, use materials from food for growth. Recall that animals' food comes from plants, other animals, or both. When an animal eats, the animal's body takes materials from the food and changes them into the different kinds of matter that the body needs.

Look at the two photos above. How does the fawn get the materials it needs to grow into an adult deer?

How does the plant get the materials it needs to grow?

How are the needs of the fawn and the plant similar?

Animals also need materials to repair their bodies if they are injured. If you get a cut, your body must be able to heal itself. A scab will form over the wound for protection. Then new skin will form under the scab.

Where do the new materials to form the scab and the new skin come from?

Draw a diagram showing how food, materials, and energy are related.

Go Further

Study the photos above. What is different between the two settings for these vegetable plants?

Water and air supply most of the materials that plants need to live and grow. But plants do get some nutrients from soil. These nutrients are materials that plants need in very small amounts. Farmers usually grow plants in soil. But sometimes farmers grow plants without soil. Plants are placed in a system in which nutrients are added to the water that is given to the plants. The plants take in the nutrients as they take in water through their roots.

Plants can be grown without soil. Do you think plants can also be grown without air? Explain your answer.

Check Your Understanding

1 A 21-gram melon seedling was planted in some rich soil in the ground. The plant was watered on a regular basis. After 30 days, the plant had grown to 100 grams. Which statement is true?

A ☐ The plant got all the materials it needed to grow from water.

B ☐ The plant got the materials it needed to grow mainly from air and water.

C ☐ The plant grew by using materials only from the soil.

D ☐ The plant grew by using materials only from the air.

2 An eagle, a tree, and an air plant live in the same area. Compare what the organisms need in order to grow. Mark an X in the box for each material the organism needs.

	Eagle	Tree	Air Plant
Soil			
Air			
Water			
Food source			

3 An orchid is growing on a branch of a large tree. The orchid is an air plant. How does this plant get the materials it needs in order to grow?

_____

_____

_____

4 A girl plants a tree in her backyard. Over several years, the tree grows larger. The girl grows as well. Explain how the growth of the girl and the tree are similar. Then explain the differences between what each of them needs in order to grow.

_____

_____

_____

_____

5 In the space below, draw a model to show how a tree gets the materials it needs in order to grow. Use your explanation above and what you have learned to label the parts of your model.

How Matter Moves through Ecosystems

Look closely at the photos.

Discuss the photos with a partner. What do you think is happening to the fruit in these photos? Record your ideas below.

Describe a time you have seen something like this happen in real life.

Believe it or not, the growth you see on the apple and on the orange is alive. It is helping to break the fruit down.

Look at the two photos. Compare the fallen tree to the growing tree. What changes are happening to each tree?

Think about the photos on the previous page. How are the changes that are happening to the fallen tree like the changes that are happening to the fruit?

Look Ahead

Every ecosystem has living things that break down the remains of other living things. In this lesson, you will learn how these recyclers work.

Explore!

Earthworm Observations

Materials

- Live earthworms
- Paper towels
- Hand lenses
- Clear plastic cup
- Soil
- Colored pencils or crayons

Steps

1 Your teacher will give your group an earthworm to observe. Gently put your earthworm on a paper towel. Use a hand lens to observe the earthworm. Draw a picture of the earthworm in the space below.

2 Fill the clear plastic cup at least halfway with soil. Carefully pick up the paper towel and put the earthworm in the cup on top of the soil.

Safety First!
Use caution when handling living things. Be careful not to harm them.

3 Using a hand lens, observe the earthworm for at least five minutes.

4 What did the earthworm do? Record your observations below. Then draw a picture to show your observation of the earthworm in the soil.

_____

_____

5 What happened to the soil when the earthworm was placed in the cup?

_____

_____

Think About It

Think about how earthworms may help break down leaves that drop from trees in fall. Record your ideas below.

As the earthworm moves, it loosens the soil. This allows water and other nutrients to flow through the soil more easily. With that in mind, think about how earthworms may help new plants grow. Record your ideas below.

Understand

What happens to an organism that dies but is not eaten? It is broken down by living things called decomposers. Decomposers survive by breaking down dead organisms or waste produced by living things. Decomposers use some of this material for nutrients to live and grow. The rest of this material becomes part of the soil.

Consumers break down food inside their bodies. Unlike consumers, decomposers break down food outside their bodies. Then decomposers take in the nutrients they need.

The two main groups of decomposers are fungi and bacteria. Fungi, such as mushrooms, decompose mostly dead plants. Bacteria decompose mostly dead animals. A few animals, such as earthworms, can also act as decomposers. Earthworms break down mainly plant material. Look at the picture of some decomposers below.

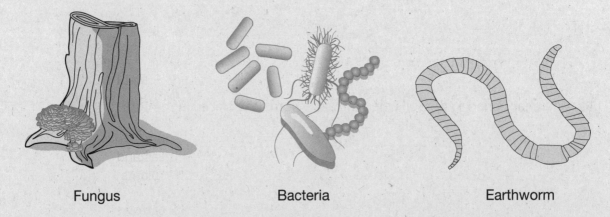

| Fungus | Bacteria | Earthworm |

Think back to the Explore activity. What other function do earthworms perform?

You observed a photo of a fallen tree earlier in this lesson. Look back at that photo now. What type of fungi is growing on the fallen tree?

In an ecosystem, matter moves between the air and soil and among plants, animals, and decomposers. Organisms take in gases that they need from the air. They get food and water from their environment. Then, they release waste matter into the environment. All organisms eventually die. Their waste matter and their remains decompose in the soil. In this way, some materials are returned to the soil. Plants take in some of these materials and change them into food that they need.

Decomposers help keep the soil in an ecosystem healthy. They are nature's recyclers. They return the nutrients from dead organisms back to the soil. Decomposers are helpful to the whole ecosystem because plants need some of these nutrients to grow.

The cycling of nutrients is essential to an ecosystem. This is because most organisms can trace their food source back to plants. The diagram below shows a food web. A food web is a model that shows how matter moves through an ecosystem.

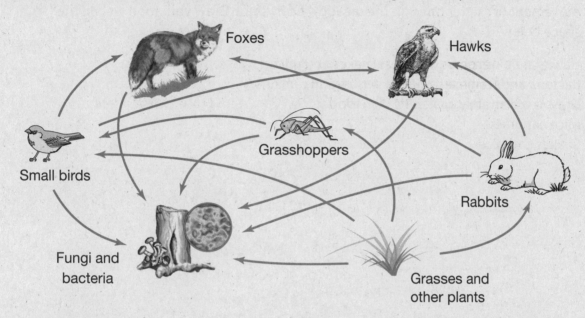

Put your finger on any animal in the food web above and follow the arrows backward. You will end up where all food webs begin—with a producer. You can see that the producers in this ecosystem are plants. No matter what an animal eats, the nutrients in its food began with a plant. The nutrients that almost all animals get from their food can be traced back to plant matter.

Trace the flow of matter and energy from a hawk through the ecosystem shown above. Where does the hawk get the nutrients it needs to live and grow?

How does the hawk return matter to the rest of the ecosystem?

A food web focuses on a single ecosystem. It lets you trace the flow of matter from plants, through many animals, and to decomposers. All food webs end with decomposers. Decomposers keep ecosystems clean by breaking down wastes and remains. They return this matter to the soil.

The information below describes some of the organisms in a meadow ecosystem. Use the information to create a food web. The food web you create will be a model of the movement of matter through the meadow ecosystem. Draw your food web in the space below.

Hawks are birds of prey that eat snakes and mice.
Bacteria and fungi decompose wastes and remains.
Grass is a plant that makes its own food.
Mice eat grass.
Snakes eat mice.

Are decomposers an important part of the food web of the meadow ecosystem? Explain.

Go Further

In an earlier lesson, you learned that a food chain can model how energy from the sun cycles through living things. A food chain can also model how matter cycles through living things. Look at the food chain below.

Plant   Caterpillar   Bird   Fox   Bacteria

In this food chain, the plant is a producer. The caterpillar eats the plant. A bird eats the caterpillar. Then a fox eats the bird. When the fox dies, decomposers break down its remains. A food chain starts with a producer and ends with a decomposer.

Several food chains connect to form a food web. A food web also starts with a producer and ends with a decomposer. But a food web is more complicated. The food web you studied earlier in the lesson is shown again below. The grasshoppers are not the only ones that eat plants. The rabbits and small birds eat plants, too. The rabbits and small birds, in turn, are eaten by both foxes and hawks. The fungi and bacteria return nutrients to the soil from wastes and the remains of plants and animals that die.

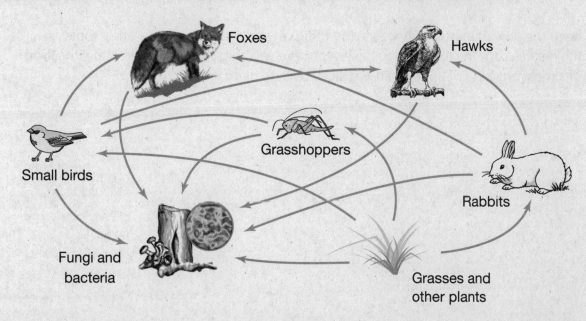

Foxes   Hawks

Grasshoppers

Small birds   Rabbits

Fungi and bacteria   Grasses and other plants

Identify three food chains in the food web above. Each food chain will start with a producer and end with a decomposer. Fill in the organisms' names below.

_____ → _____ → _____

_____ → _____ → _____

_____ → _____ → _____

Rub a piece of bread around on a dusty windowsill. Place the bread on a plate, and wrap it with plastic wrap. Leave the bread there for a few days. Observe the bread each day. What changes do you see? Explain what you think is happening to the bread.

_____

_____

_____

Think about the photos of the fruit from the beginning of the lesson. How do you think the process happening to your bread relates to those photos?

_____

_____

_____

Keep the flow of matter between living things in mind as you explore other topics in the next lesson. The models you have seen here will help you understand how the food of almost any kind of animal can be traced back to plant matter.

Check Your Understanding

1 Which of the following is **not** true of a food web?

   A ⬜ It begins with plants that produce their own food.

   B ⬜ It includes plants and animals.

   C ⬜ It is only between plants and animals.

   D ⬜ Decomposers are a part of it.

2 Select all the decomposers listed below.

   A ⬜ bacteria

   B ⬜ earthworm

   C ⬜ grass

   D ⬜ hawk

   E ⬜ mushroom

   F ⬜ rabbit

3 Explain what is happening to the dinner roll in the photo below.

_____

_____

_____

4   The information below describes how matter moves through an ocean ecosystem. Use the information to develop a food web to model the movement of matter through this ecosystem. Draw your food web in the space below.

Bacteria and fungi decompose wastes and remains.
Phytoplankton are tiny ocean plants.
Whales eat phytoplankton.
Small fish, such as herring, eat phytoplankton.
Birds eat small fish.
Large fish eat small fish.
Seals eat small fish.
Sharks eat small fish, large fish, and seals.

5   Look at the food web you made. Explain how sharks, bacteria, seals, and small fish are all related.

_____

_____

_____

Lesson 9

Healthy Ecosystems

Look closely at the photos.

Discuss these photos with a partner. How are the three photos related? Record your ideas below.

Look at the photos again. What do all animals need to survive? Record your ideas.

Sometimes environments can change. These changes have an effect on all the living things in that environment. Some changes make it harder for living things to survive.

Look at the photo of the bird feeding its baby chicks in their nest. What would happen to the birds if there were no trees for a nest?

Look again at the photo of the leopard. How does the leopard get what it needs from the environment to survive?

Look Ahead

Living things can only survive in an environment that meets their needs. What happens to living things when the environment changes? This is a question that you will start to explore in this lesson.

Explore!

Ecosystem Research

Materials

- Reference materials provided by your teacher
- Pencil and paper
- Colored pencils or crayons

Steps

1 Record the type of ecosystem assigned to your group on the line below.

_____

2 Use the reference materials that your teacher provided to do research on your assigned ecosystem. Find out about the characteristics of the ecosystem. Use what you find to describe the ecosystem on the lines below. Then draw a picture of the ecosystem.

_____

_____

_____

_____

3 With your group, choose five organisms that can be found in your ecosystem. Be sure to include both plants and animals. In the table below, list each of the five organisms in the first column. Then complete the table by describing each organism.

Organism	Description of Organism
1.	
2.	
3.	
4.	
5.	

4 How do the organisms in this ecosystem get what they need from their environment?

_____

_____

Think About It

What do all living things need to get from their environment?

Understand

When you worked with your group to find the plants and animals that live in an ecosystem, you were using a healthy ecosystem as a model. A healthy ecosystem is needed for all organisms to survive.

A healthy ecosystem provides everything that an organism needs to live and grow. It provides food and water for plants and animals. It provides space for plants to grow and shelter for animals.

Look at the photo of an ecosystem above. Describe the ecosystem. Describe ways in which the living things in this healthy ecosystem can meet their needs.

What could an animal use for shelter in this healthy ecosystem?

Ecosystems can change. Some changes are normal and occur in nature all the time. Disease can cause a whole group of plants or animals to die. A flood can carry away the soil that plants need to grow. This can make it difficult for animals to find food. A forest destroyed by fire takes a long time to recover and grow new plants and trees. An earthquake can cause permanent changes to the land.

Humans also cause changes to ecosystems. When people build new towns, they cut down trees and take away the sources of food and shelter that animals need. Pollution from factories can poison river water. These changes make it difficult for some plants and animals to survive.

Changes to an ecosystem can have an effect on all the plants and animals in that ecosystem.

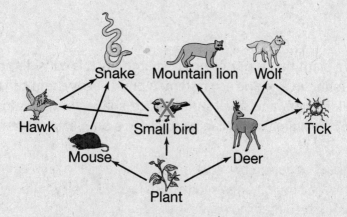

Look at the illustration above. The plants and animals live in the same ecosystem. Most of the small birds died due to disease.

What impact does the loss of the small birds have on the plants and the other animals in the ecosystem?

Are all animals in the ecosystem affected by the loss of the small birds? Explain your answer.

An ecosystem also changes when a new species of plant or animal is introduced. This can upset the balance in an ecosystem. Sometimes when a new plant is introduced, the new plant takes over more and more space. The new plant may use most of the water and sunlight that other plants need. The other plants no longer have access to the resources they need to survive. The new plant survives and the other plants die.

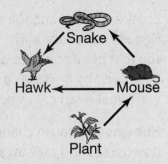

What could happen to the mice, hawks, and snakes in the food web shown above if the plant that the mice eat is replaced with another type of plant?

Poison hemlock is a plant that is poisonous to mammals. It is considered to be a weed and is sometimes found in a prairie ecosystem. A prairie ecosystem can include plants such as grasses, wildflowers, and small shrubs. Mice, snakes, birds, prairie dogs, coyotes, and elk are some of the animals that can be found in a prairie ecosystem.

Think about the impact of poison hemlock on the prairie ecosystem. What could happen to the other plants? What could happen to the animals? Record your answer below. Then draw a model of a food web that shows the impact.

Go Further

In 1989, an oil tanker called the *Exxon Valdez* had an accident off the coast of Alaska. The result was that about 11 million gallons of oil were spilled into the Pacific Ocean. About 1300 miles of ocean shoreline had some damage from the oil. Many animals and plants died as a result of the oil spill.

Look at the photos above. Many sea otters and seagulls live along the coast of Alaska. How do you think the oil spill affected these animals?

What effect do you think the oil spill had on plants, both in the ocean and on the shore?

Ecosystems can be disrupted when a new animal is introduced. Sometimes people bring an animal into an area where it does not belong. The animal uses resources that other animals need to survive. One such animal is the Burmese python.

Burmese pythons are snakes that are found naturally in Southeast Asia. They were brought to the United States to sell as pets. Some pet owners released the snakes into the wild when they became too much to care for. Many of the pythons were released into the Florida Everglades. There is no animal in the Everglades that preys on pythons. So the population of pythons has grown. The pythons prey on the other animals in the ecosystem. As a result, the populations of deer, raccoons, marsh rabbits, bobcats, and opossums in this ecosystem have decreased.

Burmese pythons have become a huge problem for the Everglades ecosystem. What ideas do you have for restoring the natural balance in this ecosystem? Record your ideas below.

Try This

The Florida Everglades is a large wetlands ecosystem. Use what you have learned about ecosystems and reference materials about the Florida Everglades to learn more about wetlands ecosystems. On a separate sheet of paper, describe a wetlands ecosystem such as the Florida Everglades. Then draw a picture of the ecosystem.

Check Your Understanding

1 What do organisms need from their ecosystem to survive? Select all that apply.

A ◯ food

B ◯ buildings

C ◯ fire

D ◯ floods

E ◯ shelter

F ◯ water

2 Match each item in the box to one of the descriptions. Write the letter of the correct choice on each line.

A. Ecosystem	B. Shelter	C. Food web

_____ A place for an animal that is safe from danger and bad weather

_____ A system of all the living and nonliving things in an area

_____ A model that shows how energy moves from one organism to another in an ecosystem

3 Which word describes a human-made change to an ecosystem?

A ◯ disease

B ◯ pollution

C ◯ flood

D ◯ earthquake

4   Look at the food chain below.

A Food Chain

mountain lion

raccoon

mouse   grass

What would happen to the other organisms in the food chain if all the raccoons died off from disease?

_____

_____

_____

_____

5   Name one type of pollution. How can pollution affect an organism and its ecosystem?

_____

_____

_____

_____

The Sun-Earth-Moon System

You look pretty good for someone who is hurtling through space all the time.

Earth moves around the sun, and the moon moves around Earth. Earth also spins like a top. These motions don't make us dizzy. But they do make things look different to us at different times of day and different times of year. Have you noticed?

By the end of this unit, you will be able to answer some big questions. Why can we feel and see the sun during the day but not at night? If there are billions of stars in the sky, why can't we feel their heat? Why does the sun appear to move across the sky? Why do shadows get shorter and longer during the day?

Next time you are outside, see what you notice.

Lesson 10

The Sun

Look at the photo. Think about what it shows.

On a cloudless night, you can see many stars. The stars appear as tiny points of light in the dark sky. Look closely at the stars in the photo. How do the stars appear different from one another? Record your ideas below.

Why do you think the stars appear different from one another? Record your ideas.

The cluster of stars in the photo that looks like a band of light is part of the Milky Way galaxy. A galaxy is a group of billions of stars held together by gravity.

It may surprise you to learn that the sun is a star. The sun certainly does not look like the stars you see at night. The sun is one of many stars in the Milky Way galaxy.

What do you already know about the sun and other stars? Record your ideas below.

Why do you think the sun looks so different from the other stars in the photo? Record your ideas.

Look Ahead

The brightness of the sun is very different from other stars. The distance of the sun from Earth is also much different when compared to other stars. You will investigate and compare the brightness and distance of the sun with other stars in this lesson.

Explore!

Comparing Brightness and Distance

Materials

- 2 small flashlights with AA batteries
- 1 large flashlight with D batteries
- Tape
- Two 8 cm × 15 cm strips of paper
- One 8 cm × 20 cm strip of paper

Steps

1. Work in a small group. Roll one 8 cm × 15 cm strip of paper into a tube and tape the tube around the lighted end of a small flashlight. Do the same with the other small flashlight.

2. The group should position themselves 30 cm from the wall. Have one group member shine one of the small flashlights straight forward onto the wall. From the same distance, have another group member shine the second small flashlight straight forward onto the same wall. Record your observations about the brightness of each flashlight.

   _____

   _____

   _____

3. Next, have one of the group members who is shining a small flashlight onto the dark wall step back about ten steps. The other group member stays in place (30 cm from the wall). Record your observations about the brightness of the two flashlights.

   _____

   _____

   _____

4 Roll the 8 cm × 20 cm strip of paper into a tube. Tape the tube around the lighted end of the large flashlight. Repeat Step 2 using the large flashlight and only one of the small flashlights. Have two group members shine the flashlights straight forward onto the dark wall from a distance of 30 cm. Record your observations.

_____

_____

5 Have the group member who is holding the large flashlight move ten steps back. The other group member stays in place (30 cm from the wall). Record your observations about the brightness of the two flashlights.

_____

_____

Think About It

Think about what you observed with the two small flashlights. How can you explain what you observed when one of the small flashlights was ten steps back from the other?

Think about what you observed with the small and large flashlights. How can you explain what you observed when the large flashlight was ten steps back from the small flashlight?

Understand

The sun is a star, a giant sphere of gases that produces light and heat. The sun is the closest star to Earth and the only star in our solar system. Because the sun is much closer than other stars, it looks much larger and brighter than other stars. A star that looks small and dim from Earth may actually be larger and brighter than the sun. The star appears to us to be small and dim because it is so far away.

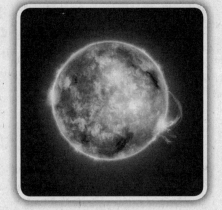

All stars give off heat, but only the sun's heat reaches Earth. The stars that you see at night continue to shine during the day. However, the sun's light is much brighter than the light from more distant stars. That is why you cannot see other stars during the day.

Of all the known stars, some are larger than the sun and some are smaller. Compared with other stars, the sun is an average-size star. Stars may be white, yellow, orange, or even blue.

Light travels through space. We can see the light that travels to Earth from the stars. Light from the sun takes only about eight minutes to reach Earth. Light from other stars takes many years to reach Earth because the other stars are so far away.

Imagine you are riding a spaceship across the solar system. How would the size of the sun appear to change as you travel from Earth to the end of the solar system? Use words and pictures to show the apparent change in the size of the sun.

Stars are clustered into large groups called *galaxies*. The sun is part of the Milky Way galaxy. Scientists estimate that there are between one hundred billion and four hundred billion stars in the Milky Way galaxy. You can see stars in the Milky Way galaxy from Earth. But most of the stars in other galaxies are too far away from Earth to see without a very powerful telescope. The diagram below shows the sun's location in the Milky Way. The sun would be only a very tiny dot in the diagram.

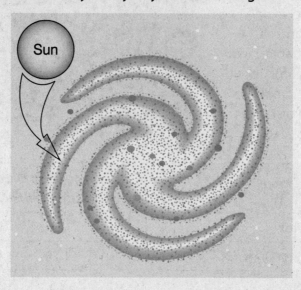

Think about what you have learned about how their distance from Earth affects the appearance of the sun and other stars. How do your observations from the Explore activity support your answer?

Science Tools

Stars are very large, but they are very far away. This makes them difficult to observe. Scientists can view stars with optical telescopes. These telescopes use a series of glass lenses that gather and focus light. They make objects appear larger. This allows scientists to observe details of objects that are far away.

Go Further

Stars vary greatly in their distances from Earth. In the photo shown here, some of the stars are closer to Earth than others. The distance of stars from Earth is measured in light-years. One light-year is the distance light can travel in one year, or about 9.5 trillion kilometers. Traveling that fast, you could circle Earth's equator about 7.5 times in just one second! The table below shows the distances of some stars from Earth.

Star	Distance from Earth in Light-Years
Pollux	34
Sigma Draconis	18.8
Sirius	8.6
Alpha Centauri	4.4
Arcturus	37

Study the light-year distances in the table. Then draw a model showing Earth and the stars in the table in order of nearest to farthest distance from Earth. In your model, label Earth and each of the stars.

The table of stars on the previous page showed five stars and their approximate distances from Earth. The stars are far away from Earth. The table below shows four more stars and their approximate distances from Earth. The four stars in the table below are much farther from Earth. Choose one of the stars from the previous page and one of the stars below to show in a distance model. Draw the distance model showing how far each star is from Earth by using this scale: 1 mm = 10 light-years (1 cm = 100 light-years).

Star	Distance from Earth in Light-Years
Spica	260
Becrux	460
Adhara	430
Betelgeuse	640

How does your model support what you learned about the distance of stars from Earth?

1 Why does the sun appear larger than other stars?

   A ◯ It is hotter than other stars.

   B ◯ It is much larger than other stars.

   C ◯ It is closer to Earth than other stars.

   D ◯ It is brighter than other stars.

2 Why are the stars that appear in the night sky not visible during the day?

   A ◯ The sun's light is too bright.

   B ◯ The stars do not produce light during the day.

   C ◯ The stars turn away from Earth during the day.

   D ◯ Earth moves farther away from the stars during the day.

3 Four stars are of equal size. Their distances in light-years from Earth are shown in the table below.

Star	Distance from Earth in Light-Years
A	250
B	67
C	120
D	34

Which will most likely appear to be the brightest of the four stars when you look at the night sky from Earth?

   A ◯ Star A

   B ◯ Star B

   C ◯ Star C

   D ◯ Star D

4   Think about what you observed and learned from the photos and the Explore activity in this lesson. How do stars' distances from Earth help explain that stars in the night sky seem to differ in size and brightness? Use evidence from the Explore activity and the text to support your answer.

_____

_____

_____

_____

5   A friend says that a star that gives off a greater amount of light will always look brighter from Earth than one that gives off a lesser amount of light. Do you agree? Why or why not?

_____

_____

_____

_____

Lesson 11

Day and Night, Shadows, and the Night Sky

Look closely at the picture.

In the future, an astronaut might have this view from space. Discuss what you see with your group. Record your observations below.

At what time of day would you see each of these objects in the sky? Record your answer.

Look carefully at the photo. The photo was taken in a park. Discuss the photo with your group.

What do you see in the photo? When would you see what is shown in the photo?

Look Ahead

Standing on Earth, it may not feel like you are traveling through space. But you are. Earth moves around the sun. The moon circles Earth. Do they move in a regular way? If so, do they move in patterns that we can see? You will explore these questions in this lesson.

Explore!

Making Night and Day

Materials

- World globe mounted on a stand
- Flashlight
- Small ball
- Metric ruler
- Small piece of modeling clay
- Toothpick

Steps

1 Place the globe on a table. Hold the flashlight about 60 cm away from one side of the globe, and shine the light on the globe. Where does the light strike the globe?

_____

2 Slowly spin the globe while shining the light on it from the same distance. Can the flashlight light up the entire globe at one time? How much of the globe has light striking it?

_____

Safety First!

Be careful not to shine the flashlight into your own eyes or anyone else's eyes.

3 Locate where you live on the globe. Place a small piece of clay there, and stick a toothpick in it. This marks your hometown. Shine the flashlight on the globe, and spin the globe until your hometown is in the light. Use the space below to draw a picture of the globe, showing what part of the globe is in light and what part is in shadow. In your drawing, label your hometown. Then label a city, country, or continent on the side of the globe that is in shadow.

4 Put the globe aside. Then place the ball on the table. Look at the diagram below. The gray circle represents the ball resting on the table.

A

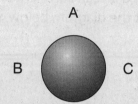

B   C

Hold the flashlight about 20 cm from the ball. Shine the light on the ball from each position shown in the diagram. The *A* position is directly above the ball. The *B* and *C* positions are at the sides of the ball. Use the ruler to measure the length of any shadows. Fill in the table below by recording your data and observations.

Flashlight Position	Shadow (Yes/No)	Length of Shadow (in centimeters)	Direction of Shadow
A			
B			
C			

Think About It

Look at the data and observations you recorded in your table. Did holding the flashlight and shining light on the ball from positions *B* and *C* cause shadows of similar length? Did holding the flashlight and shining light on the ball from positions *B* and *C* cause shadows to appear in the same direction? Explain your answers below.

Understand

Like all planets in our solar system, Earth travels around the sun in a nearly circular path. The amount of time Earth takes to complete its path around the sun is about 365 days. This period of time is called a year. Earth is at about the same place in its path at the same time each year. Look at the diagram below, which shows Earth at different points in its path around the sun.

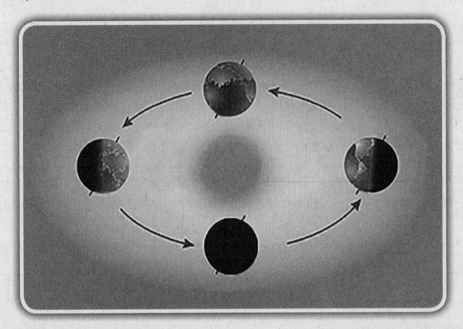

Do you think Earth is in the same place on the first day of summer each year? Explain your answer.

In the diagram above, Earth looks like a round ball because it is shaped like a sphere. The diagram shows the imaginary line running up through the middle of Earth. This line is called Earth's axis. The North Pole is at one end of the axis. The South Pole is at the opposite end of the axis. Earth turns constantly on its axis, like a spinning top.

Recall the Explore activity. How did the globe in the activity model Earth?

Think about the difference between day and night. What is the main difference between them? The main difference between day and night is whether or not there is light from the sun. There is light from the sun during the day, but not at night. Even on cloudy days when the bright sun is not visible, it still lights the sky. This does not mean that at night the sun has disappeared or that it has stopped shining. The sun is still shining even during the darkest nights, but it is not visible from some parts of Earth.

As Earth spins on its axis, different places on its surface receive the sun's light. At any given time, the half of Earth's surface that is facing the sun is receiving light—in the same way that half of the globe's surface in the Explore activity was receiving light from the flashlight. The other half of Earth is facing away from the sun. In these places, it is night.

Recall that Earth spins constantly on its axis. When it is daytime where you are, Earth has spun so that you are facing the sun. When it is nighttime, Earth has spun so that you are facing away from the sun. Earth makes one complete turn on its axis every 24 hours. That 24-hour period is one day.

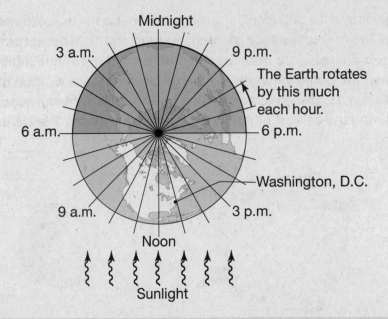

On the diagram above, find the place where you live. According to the diagram, what time is it there? Estimate the time to the nearest half hour. In how many hours will it be nighttime there, according to the diagram?

During the morning, the sun appears to rise in the sky. By midday, the sun appears to reach its highest point in the sky and may seem to be directly overhead. As the day continues, the sun seems to move lower and lower across the sky. When the sun has gone down completely, it is night again. The sun is not moving around Earth—although it might look that way. It is Earth that is spinning, and its motion causes day and night.

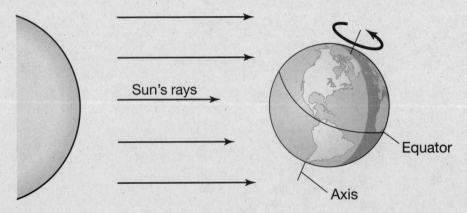

On a sunny day, objects cast shadows. The shadows cast by objects also change as Earth turns. Remember when you used a flashlight to cast shadows on the ball that represented Earth in the Explore activity? You saw that the position of a shadow changed with the position of the flashlight. In the same way, the position of a shadow changes with the position of the sun in the sky. In the illustration below, notice the position of the sun and the shadows that are created at different times of the day.

Using the illustration above and your investigation with the flashlight in the Explore activity, where is the sun when the shadows are shortest? Where is the sun when the shadows are longest?

Look back at the data table you completed in the Explore activity. In the space below, make a bar graph to show shadow length measurements. Label the bottom axis *A*, *B*, and *C*. Show a scale of your centimeter measurements along the other axis.

Go Further

The moon travels with Earth around the sun. The moon also moves around Earth in a circular path. It takes the moon about 30 days to complete this path around Earth. A month was originally based on the number of days the moon takes to move around Earth.

Draw a diagram in the box below to show the moon circling around Earth as Earth is circling around the sun.

Just like Earth, the moon spins on an axis. It takes the moon about 30 days to spin once on its axis. The moon also takes 30 days to circle once around Earth. The result is that we always see the same side of the moon.

About how many times does the moon circle Earth during the one year it takes for Earth to circle the sun? Explain how you reached your conclusion.

You may have noticed that you see different stars in the night sky at different times of year. That is because Earth faces different parts of the sky as it moves around the sun.

In ancient times, people thought they recognized patterns in the stars of the night sky. They imagined pictures of gods, people in stories, animals, or other objects in groups of stars they saw. These groups of stars became known as constellations.

On a dark night, constellations fill the night sky. But the constellations you see in summer are not the same as those you see in winter. Different constellations appear overhead at different times of year because Earth is at different places in its path around the sun. The star chart below shows the night sky in winter for people on Earth who live north of the equator. Constellations are shown by the lines connecting certain groups of stars.

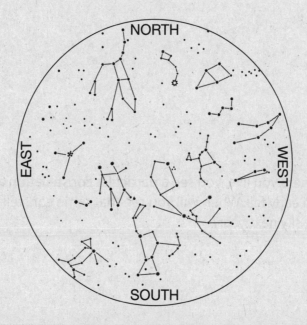

Would you expect the star chart to be the same next winter? Explain your answer.

Do you think the star chart for summer looks like the star chart for winter? Explain your answer.

1 Select each sentence that is true about shadows after about 4:00 p.m. each day.

   A ◯ They are long.

   B ◯ They are short.

   C ◯ They point in two different directions.

   D ◯ They will get longer as the day continues.

   E ◯ They will get shorter as the day continues.

2 How long does it take for Earth to complete its nearly circular path around the sun?

   A ◯ a day

   B ◯ a week

   C ◯ a month

   D ◯ a year

3 This year, from where you live, you see a particular constellation at a certain place in the night sky in early fall. When will you see that same constellation at the same place in the night sky next year?

   A ◯ late winter

   B ◯ early fall

   C ◯ late fall

   D ◯ early spring

4 How many times does the moon circle around the sun in one year? Explain your answer.

_____

_____

_____

_____

5 If the sun does not circle Earth, why does it appear to rise, move across the sky, and then set each day?

_____

_____

_____

_____

Earth's Systems

Why is Earth sometimes called the Blue Planet? That is not a riddle. Earth is called the Blue Planet because 71 percent of it is covered by water. Take a look at a globe.

But water alone is not enough to sustain life on Earth. In this unit, you will discover how Earth's systems work together. You will find out why we need all of them—and why we need them all to be healthy.

Human activities are not always good for the health of Earth's systems. But humans can also protect those systems. How can we meet our needs without harming the systems on which all living things depend? This unit will help you think about that question.

Lesson 12

What Are Earth's Systems?

Look at the photos above.

What do the photos show? Discuss your ideas with a partner. Then record your ideas on the lines below.

Think about what would happen if you visited the places shown in the photos. What would you see and feel in each of these places?

When you step outside, what do you observe around you? You might feel rocky ground or soil under your feet, and you might see a snow-covered mountain. You might see a lake or hear a river running close by. You might feel a breeze on your face and see clouds in the sky. You might see grass, trees, birds, and people. These things are all part of Earth's four main systems—land, water, air, and all living things.

Look closely at the photo above. How many of Earth's systems can you observe in this photo? Name something in the photo that represents each system you see.

Look Ahead

Earth has several systems that make up its natural environment. You will find out more about each of these systems in this lesson.

Explore!

Making a Terrarium

Materials

- Large glass jar with a lid
- Small pebbles
- Activated charcoal
- Potting soil
- Small plants
- Water
- Metric ruler

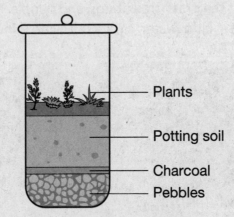

Plants

Potting soil

Charcoal

Pebbles

Steps

1. Cover the bottom of the jar with a layer of pebbles. The layer of pebbles should be about 2.5 cm deep.

2. Add a layer of activated charcoal on top of the pebbles. This layer should be about 1.25 cm deep.

3. Add a layer of soil on top of the charcoal. This layer should fill the jar about halfway.

Why do you think the soil is put on top of layers of charcoal and pebbles?

4. Your teacher will give you the plants for your terrarium. Use your fingers to make a small hole in the soil for each plant. Put the roots of each plant gently into a hole. Then gently push the soil around the plant and cover the roots completely. Be sure to leave some space between the plants.

5. Water the plants, but do not soak them.

6. Cover your terrarium with a lid. Your teacher will assist you in placing your terrarium in a well-lit location.

Think About It

Think about how the terrarium models Earth's systems. Record your thoughts below.

Share your thoughts with your group. Then listen to their ideas. Use the lines below if you want to revise your ideas.

Understand

Earth is a sphere, or a solid round object, and the terms we use for each of its four main systems are made up from the base word *sphere*. The geosphere is the rock and soil of Earth's surface. The hydrosphere is Earth's waters. The atmosphere is the layer of air that surrounds Earth. The biosphere is made up of living things. In the Explore activity, you made a terrarium. You learned that all four of Earth's main systems were represented in the terrarium. You can also observe each of these natural systems in the diagram below.

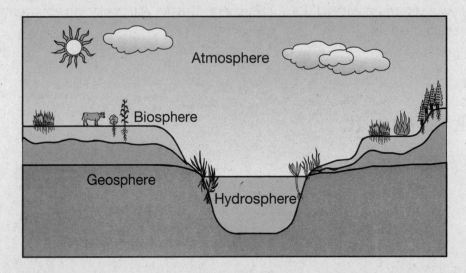

Use the diagram to fill out the table below with the names of Earth's natural systems.

Earth's Natural Systems

System (Sphere) Name	What It Is
	Earth's rocky surface and soil
	Earth's waters
	The layer of air that surrounds Earth
	All the living things on Earth

The geosphere is the solid part of Earth. It is Earth's rocky surface. It is also the soil and sediments that cover Earth. The landforms of the geosphere change over time. Some changes are fast—like a volcanic eruption that blows the top off a mountain. Other changes are slow. Weathering and erosion slowly wear away rock over many years.

Think back to the Explore activity. How might the parts of the terrarium change over time?

Earth's waters are the hydrosphere. The hydrosphere, like the geosphere, is part of Earth's surface. Earth is sometimes called the "water planet" because the hydrosphere covers most of its surface. Most of this water is the salty water in oceans and seas. Freshwater—water that is not salty—makes up a much smaller part of the hydrosphere. Yet freshwater is very important. It is the only type of water that we can drink.

Most of Earth's surface is covered by salt water, but we need freshwater to drink. Think back to the Explore activity. In what other ways is freshwater important to people?

Liquid freshwater is found in streams, rivers, lakes, and wetlands. A wetland is a low area that is often wet all year. Swamps and marshes are wetlands. Rain also seeps into the soil and collects under the ground as groundwater. Water is even found in the air as water vapor. But about three-fourths of Earth's freshwater is stored as ice. Frozen forms of freshwater include the polar ice caps, glaciers, and snow.

Is most of the freshwater of the hydrosphere available for use by plants and animals? Explain.

What are the two systems that make up Earth's surface? What do they represent?

You interact with one of Earth's systems each time you take a breath—the atmosphere. The atmosphere is the mixture of gases that surrounds Earth. Plants and animals on Earth need the gases in the atmosphere to live. The plants in your terrarium use the air inside it to live and make food.

Some of the gases in the atmosphere help keep us warm. They hold Earth's heat near its surface, making life possible. Earth would be much colder without these gases. That is why they are called greenhouse gases. Like the glass walls of a greenhouse, they trap heat.

The atmosphere also protects Earth's living things. Most living things need energy from the sun. Yet the sun contains harmful radiation. The gases in the atmosphere shield Earth from most of this harmful radiation.

Describe two ways that the atmosphere helps us.

The biosphere is all the living things on Earth. That includes all of Earth's plants and animals. People are part of the biosphere. The biosphere is part of each of the other three systems as well. Some living things, such as plants, grow in the soil of the geosphere. Other living things, such as fish, swim through the waters of the hydrosphere. Many living things, such as plants and animals, including people, also spend much of their lives in the atmosphere. Birds and many insects even fly in the atmosphere.

What are two ways that the biosphere is different from the geosphere?

Go Further

You have learned why Earth is considered to be a water planet—because the hydrosphere covers most of its surface. Look at the chart below. It shows the distribution of water on Earth.

All Water

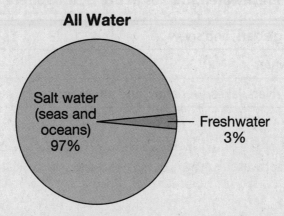

Salt water (seas and oceans) 97%

Freshwater 3%

What part of the water on Earth's surface is salt water? How does that compare to the amount of freshwater? Record your ideas below.

Only a small percentage of the hydrosphere is freshwater. The table below shows the main sources of freshwater.

Freshwater Sources in the Hydrosphere

Ice caps, glaciers, and snow	69%
Groundwater	30%
Streams, rivers, lakes, wetlands, and atmosphere	1%

Use the information in the table to draw a circle graph in the space below. Your graph should show the way freshwater is split among the three sources listed in the table.

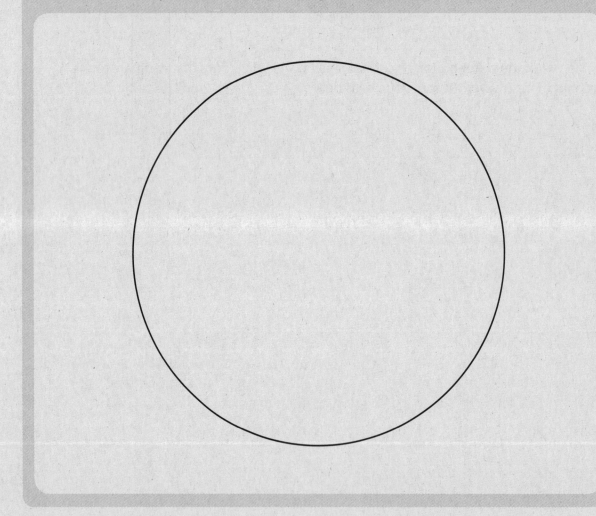

Our survival depends on interactions with all of Earth's systems.

List something important that humans get from each system. Explain why that thing is important for human survival.

Which of the photos above show the four systems of Earth? Explain your answer.

Keep what you learned about Earth's systems in mind as you explore related topics in this book. This information will help you understand more about how Earth's systems interact with each other.

1   Which of these statements **best** describes all of Earth's natural systems?

   A ◯ Earth has four systems that are all part of the geosphere.

   B ◯ The hydrosphere and geosphere are part of Earth's surface.

   C ◯ Earth has four natural systems that make up its environments.

   D ◯ The atmosphere is very important because it contains the air we breathe.

2

| **A. Freshwater** | **B. Hydrosphere** | **C. Salt water** |

Write the letter of the correct term on each line.

_____ System of all of Earth's water

_____ Water that covers most of Earth's surface

_____ Water we use most in everyday life

3   Label each of Earth's systems, or spheres, on the diagram below.

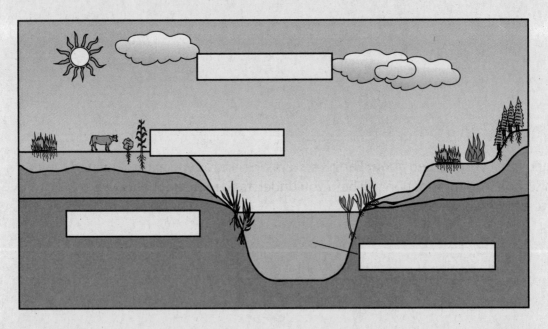

4   What makes up the geosphere? How do you think the geosphere affects life on Earth? Explain.

_____

_____

_____

_____

5   Describe what makes up the biosphere on the lines below. Then use the space to show in a drawing how the parts of the biosphere depend on Earth's other three natural systems.

_____

_____

_____

Lesson 13

How Earth's Systems Interact

Look carefully at the photos above.

How are the landscapes shown in the two photos different? Record your ideas on the lines below.

Based on the landscapes, what kind of weather do you think is common in each place? Discuss ideas about rainfall and temperature with a partner. Then record your ideas below.

You might notice the way the air feels on a certain day. Weather conditions determine the way the air feels. Weather conditions can change from day to day, or even from hour to hour. Climate is not determined by short-term changes. Climate is determined by patterns of weather over a long period of time.

Think about the two landscape photos you observed. How do you think the climate in the place shown in the photo on the left is different from the climate in the place shown in the photo on the right? Explain.

Look Ahead

Have you ever wondered why climates are so different around the world? Earth is a system with many different parts, or components. You have already learned about some of Earth's systems. As you explore this lesson, you will learn how the interaction of these systems determines climate and other Earth processes.

Explore!

Earth Systems Interaction Model

Materials

- 50 ml hot water
- Ice cubes
- Can of aerosol spray
- Glass jar with lid

Steps

1 Remove the lid from the glass jar. Pour 50 ml of hot water into the jar. Replace the lid on the jar and secure it well. Then swirl the water in the jar around. What happened to the sides of the jar when you swirled the water?

_____

_____

Safety First!

Always be careful when handling hot water.

2 Remove the lid from the glass jar. Turn the lid upside down and place some ice cubes in it. Set the upside-down lid of ice cubes on top of the jar, covering the jar opening completely. What do you observe happening in the jar?

_____

_____

3 Lift an edge of the lid and quickly spray from the aerosol can into the jar. Set the upside-down lid of ice cubes on top of the jar again, covering the jar opening completely. Describe what you see happening inside the jar.

_____

_____

4 Remove the lid from the top of the jar. When you removed the lid, what happened to the substance inside?

_____

_____

Think About It

What did the substance in the jar resemble from nature? Why do you think the substance formed in the jar? Record your ideas below.

Think about the jar as a model for natural processes on Earth. What do you think each part of the model represented in an ecosystem?

Understand

Look at the diagram below.

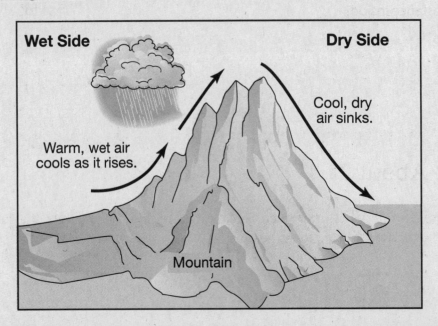

Wet Side

Dry Side

Cool, dry air sinks.

Warm, wet air cools as it rises.

Mountain

The diagram shows how water vapor rises, cools, and condenses into clouds. Where does this water vapor come from? The sun heats Earth's atmosphere. As this happens, the sun is heating the surface water of Earth's oceans, lakes, and rivers, too. Some of that surface water evaporates as water vapor and begins to rise. The air high above Earth is much colder than the air close to its surface. So the tiny droplets of water vapor begin to cool. As they cool, the droplets condense around small particles like dust in the atmosphere. The droplets gather closer together and form clouds as they continue to cool and condense. If the air is very cold, the droplets form ice crystals. Clouds are made up of billions of tiny water droplets or ice crystals, or sometimes both. Cloud formation happens because two of Earth's systems interact—the atmosphere and the hydrosphere.

Think back to the Explore activity. Do you want to revise any of your ideas about how the substance formed in the jar? Use what you have learned to explain how you modeled cloud formation.

Look again at the diagram on the previous page. Warm, wet air rises and moves up the side of the mountain. As the air moves up, it cools. Then clouds begin to form. When the water droplets in the clouds become too large and heavy, they fall as rain. Most of the rain falls on that same side of the mountain. As the cooler air sinks down on the other side of the mountain, it warms again and dries out. Places on that side of the mountain tend to have a much drier climate. These places are called *rain shadows*.

Look back at the photos you observed at the beginning of the lesson. The rain forest in the photo on the left is in western Washington State. The desertlike area shown in the photo on the right is in eastern Washington State. There is a large range of mountains between these two areas.

How can you use what you have learned about rain shadows to explain what you see in the two photos?

The hydrosphere also interacts with other Earth systems. The oceans can change the way Earth's land looks. Oceans shape landforms with their waves. The photo below shows a landform called a sea arch. Sea arches can form as ocean waves beat against a rocky shoreline. The waves erode, or wear away, bits and pieces of the landform.

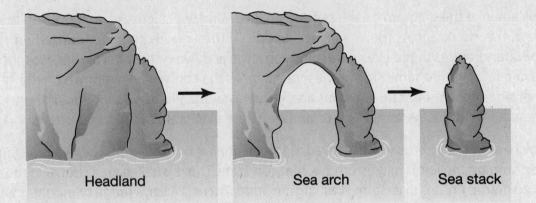

| Headland | Sea arch | Sea stack |

The diagram above models how ocean waves form a sea arch and then continue to change its shape. First, waves crack open the lower level of a rocky landform called a headland. Over time, the waves continue to beat against the crack until the rock begins to crumble and an arch is formed. The opening of the arch grows larger as the waves slam against the bottom of it. Over time, the roof of the arch will be too heavy for such a wide arch. The roof will fall, leaving a sea stack.

The ocean will continue to wear away this landform. Eventually, the sea stack will be worn away to a sea stump. Then a new crack will be opened on the landform. The process will happen again and again. As the rock formations crumble and change shape, so does the coastline. The ocean moves farther onto the shore. A continent can shrink by centimeters each year as the ocean moves farther inland.

Which two of Earth's systems interact to shape sea arches and sea stacks?

How does the ocean cause the coastline to retreat? Explain.

The hydrosphere, atmosphere, and geosphere interact to affect local and global climates. Large bodies of water, like the ocean, take in heat more slowly than land. Water also releases heat more slowly than land. In summer, ocean water takes longer to heat. The water keeps the air above it cool. In turn, the air cools nearby land. In winter, the water releases heat slowly. This heat keeps the air above the water and the nearby land warmer.

In general, will land near the ocean be colder or warmer than land far from the ocean in winter? Explain your ideas below.

Ocean water covers most of Earth's surface. This large part of the hydrosphere interacts with every other system, including the biosphere. We cannot see them all, but the ocean supports a wide variety of ecosystems. In the deep ocean ecosystem, there are giant worms and fish that can make their own light. The warm ocean surface is another ecosystem. Here, microscopic organisms make their own food, as plants do. They give off oxygen. The oxygen that these organisms produce is an important part of the atmosphere.

The photo below shows a group of tide pools. A tide pool is a puddle of water left in rocks along the shore when the ocean tide goes out. Twice a day, the ocean rises higher up on the shore and covers rocks there. Twice a day, it goes back out. Rocks that were once underwater are now exposed. Tide pools are home to a wide variety of organisms.

Some of the organisms in a tide pool ecosystem include sea stars and hermit crabs, like those shown above. These animals cling to the rocks as the waves strike them. Many organisms have shells to survive long dry periods, until they can be underwater again. The organisms must also deal with temperature changes between the air and the water.

Explain how Earth's systems interact to support the tide pool community.

Ecosystems on the shoreline are also affected by the ocean and the wind. There are several different types of plant communities along the shoreline. In a maritime forest, which is along a coast, trees are shaped by the wind and the salty air. On the side of the trees facing the ocean, the salty wind kills branches and leaves. On the other side of the same trees, leaves and branches thrive.

Explain how the biosphere and hydrosphere interact in a maritime forest.

Sand dunes are important landforms. They protect land from the ocean's water, wind, and salty air. In sand dunes, sea grasses grow long roots to anchor themselves against the wind that blows away the sand beneath them. As some plants grow taller, they block the wind for other plants to grow. Over time, the roots of the grasses hold the sand dunes in place.

Draw a model showing how the interaction of the hydrosphere, geosphere, and biosphere create sand dunes. Start your model with an ocean shoreline in the box on the left. In the following two boxes, show the changes to the shoreline as sand dunes develop.

Go Further

When Earth's systems interact, they influence weather and climate. The hydrosphere and atmosphere can influence global climates by moving heat around. When the air warms up, oceans and other bodies of water heat up as well. When warm, moist air evaporates, the process of cloud formation begins again. Areas near large bodies of water will have milder climates—warmer in winter and cooler in summer.

The photo above shows a wall of glacier ice and liquid water. At one time, the water was frozen. What would make it turn to liquid?

How do you think melting ice will influence the weather nearby?

Scientists have learned that our atmosphere has been warming over time. The illustrations below show the effect this change has had on the hydrosphere. They show the size of the polar ice cap at two different times.

Look at the illustrations above. Use the melting ice cap as a model to describe how Earth's systems interact to change the shape of landforms.

Melting polar ice caps cause the level of the ocean's water to rise. How do you think the rising water level will affect the shape of landforms and continents?

You will need two identical cups for this activity. Fill one cup with sand or soil and the other cup with water. Place the two cups in the sun for the same amount of time. After they are warm, record the temperature of each cup. Allow the cups time to cool, and record the temperature again.

What was the temperature of each cup after they sat in the sun?

Which cup cooled faster? Which had the smallest temperature change?

In this activity, you modeled how systems interact to affect climate. Explain how.

1 Select each sentence that correctly describes what happens in the creation of a rain shadow.

   A ○ Warm air cools as it drops down near a mountain and moves out over the ocean.

   B ○ Warm, wet air cools as it rises up the side of a mountain and then clouds develop.

   C ○ Both sides of a mountain tend to have a very dry climate.

   D ○ One side of a mountain tends to have a very wet climate.

   E ○ Most of the rain falls on one side of a mountain.

   F ○ Both sides of a mountain get the same amount of rain.

2 Match each item in the box to one of the descriptions. Write the letter of the correct choice on each line.

A. Atmosphere	**B. Geosphere**	**C. Biosphere**

   _____ Interacts with the hydrosphere to create and change landforms

   _____ Interacts with the hydrosphere as part of a deep ocean ecosystem

   _____ Interacts with the hydrosphere in the formation of clouds

3 Which of the following is an example of how the hydrosphere and atmosphere interact to affect climate?

   A ○ Coastal towns have colder winters than inland towns.

   B ○ Coastal mountain areas are always cool and dry in winter.

   C ○ Summers near the ocean are cooler than summers farther inland.

   D ○ Mountain areas near the ocean are always colder in winter than inland areas.

4   Look closely at the photo below.

Which of Earth's systems are interacting in the scene shown in the photo? Explain.

_____

_____

_____

5   Use the space below to draw a model of what will likely happen over time to the landform shown in the photo above.

How Humans Affect Earth's Systems

Look closely at the photos above.

What is shown in each of the photos? Discuss your observations with a partner. Record your ideas below.

Have you seen anything like what is shown in the photos near your home or in your community? Describe what you have seen. Record your ideas.

Look at the photo above. Now look again at the photos on the previous page. Are humans responsible for what is happening in each of the four photos?

Are the effects of what is happening in each photo positive or negative? Explain.

Look Ahead

Humans do many things that harm Earth's environment and resources. In this lesson, you will find out about many ways humans and communities can protect Earth.

Explore!

Reduce, Reuse, Recycle

Materials

- Plastic soda bottles
- Cardboard boxes
- Glass bottles
- Aluminum cans
- Polystyrene foam cups

Steps

1 Think about the waste, or garbage, you create in your daily life. With your group, brainstorm a list of the things from home or school that end up as waste. Record your list below.

_____

_____

_____

2 One way to reduce the amount of waste is to recycle. You might have recycling bins at home or at school like the ones shown in the photo on the right. What kinds of things do you recycle? Record your answers below.

_____

_____

_____

3 Compare your two lists. Which things on your waste list can you move to your recycle list? Record these items below.

_____

_____

_____

4 Humans can also reduce their use of Earth's resources. Talk with your group about ways you can reduce your use of resources. Record your group's ideas below.

_____

_____

_____

5 Humans can also reuse materials and products over and over again. With your group, take a look at the materials displayed by your teacher. Brainstorm different ways you can reuse the items. Think of creative ways you might use these items in your home or at school. For example, how might you use pieces of a cardboard box? Draw a picture of how you might reuse each item.

Think About It

Share and exchange your ideas with other groups. Listen to their ideas. Use the space below if you want to add to your own ideas about reusing materials.

Understand

Materials from Earth that humans use are called natural resources. These include air, water, sunlight, wind, soil, rocks, minerals, gas, coal, and oil. Plants and animals are also natural resources.

Humans use natural resources such as minerals and metal ores to make coins, steel, aluminum cans, and jewelry. Oil is used to make fuel for cars and planes, and coal is used to make electricity. Natural resources can be used in their natural forms. They can also be changed to make them more useful. For example, wood from a tree can be used to make a table or a house. Marble stone can be used in building and for sculpture. The photo below on the left shows marble stone being quarried.

Look carefully at the photo above on the right. Identify the natural resources shown. Describe a way people use each resource.

Human use of natural resources has both positive and negative effects on the environment. Fossil fuels such as coal, oil, and natural gas are natural resources used to produce energy. Burning these fuels puts harmful substances into the air. The photo below on the left shows a trainload of coal being transported from where it was mined to where it will be burned as part of the process of making electricity. The burning of coal can release pollutants into the air.

Sunlight, water, and wind are also natural resources used to produce energy. A solar array like the one in the photo above on the right can turn sunlight into electricity. Using solar power does not require burning any fossil fuels or releasing any pollutants into the air.

How is the use of coal similar to and different from the use of solar arrays?

Farmers use chemicals such as pesticides and certain kinds of fertilizers to grow crops. These chemicals can wash into streams and rivers. This is called agricultural runoff. This runoff can pollute local waterways. Runoff from sewage systems and industrial waste can also pollute Earth's waterways. Products that are no longer useful become trash. This trash may be dumped on land or in oceans. All these are forms of pollution. Pollution is the release of anything that harms the natural environment.

The factory shown in the picture below produces a product most of us use, but the waste that the factory releases is polluting a stream. Living things that live in the water may get sick or die. Animals that come to the stream to drink the water may become sick.

Some factories also produce air pollution. How do you think air pollution may affect living things in the environment?

Think back to what you wrote about the ways use of natural resources helps people but also causes harm. Record any additional ideas below.

Human activities affect natural habitats in many ways. A habitat is the place where an organism or group of organisms lives. Humans clear land to build homes and businesses. They also use land for farming. Deforestation is the continuous cutting down of forest trees without reforesting, or replanting. Deforestation destroys plant and animal habitats.

Humans use trees for lumber, paper, and other products. After a forest is cut down, the area cannot support as many organisms as it did before. Trees may grow back, but it will take many years for the area to become a mature forest again.

Think back to the photo of cut trees that you observed at the beginning of the lesson. Review the observations you wrote about that photo. Do you think deforestation has a positive or negative impact on Earth? Explain.

Using land for building, farming, or mining is called land development. When humans develop land, they remove natural resources from the area. This makes the natural habitat smaller. As a habitat gets smaller, it is more difficult for living things to find the resources they need. The living things are left without food and shelter, and they often do not survive.

What are some ways that communities can work together to prevent habitat loss and deforestation? Discuss this question with your group, and record your ideas below.

Human use of natural resources affects Earth's land, air, oceans, streams, and plant and animal habitats. Humans can use natural resources wisely so that they are not destroyed, harmed, or used up. The wise use of natural resources is called conservation. For example, we can use wind power, water power, and solar power instead of fossil fuels to meet energy needs. The wind turbines shown in the photo on the right use the power of wind to produce electricity.

Humans can also do things to restore the environment. To restore something means to put it back the way it was. Humans can plant trees. Planting trees improves the air. It also helps to prevent erosion. Humans can pick up trash. They can set aside land for parks and wilderness areas. These areas provide safe places for plants and animals.

Humans use natural resources to make products. But many natural resources are limited. Everyone can do three things to help conserve natural resources—reduce, reuse, and recycle. To reduce is to use less of something. For example, car companies can make cars that use less gasoline. To reuse is to use something again. For example, you can wash a plastic cup and use it again, instead of throwing it away. The student shown in the photo on the right is collecting old newspapers for recycling.

Think back to the Explore activity. Do you have more ideas about how you can reduce, reuse, or recycle to help conserve natural resources? Record your ideas below.

Go Further

Farmers need land to grow the food we eat. But land must be used carefully. When farmers plow the soil, it is not protected from wind and water. Wind and water can cause erosion. If wind blows away the topsoil, the land cannot be used to grow crops.

Farmers can prevent soil erosion by using methods such as contour plowing—plowing across the sides of hills instead of down their slopes. Terracing is a method in which farmers plant crops on flat terraces that are cut into hillsides.

Study the diagram below.

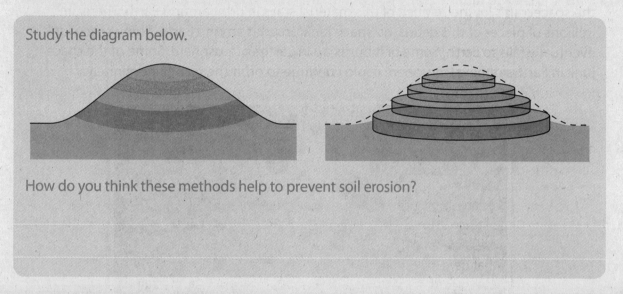

How do you think these methods help to prevent soil erosion?

Try This

Wind can cause topsoil to blow away. Design a solution for preventing wind erosion. Draw or describe your solution in the box below.

Humans send spacecraft into space to learn more about space and to deliver supplies to the International Space Station. They place satellites in orbit around Earth to map Earth and to learn more about it. Satellites also allow people to communicate across long distances.

What happens to those satellites if they break or become no longer useful? What happens to the parts of a spacecraft that break off or are ejected on purpose during the spacecraft's journey? Much of this material stays in orbit around Earth. There are millions of pieces of this debris, or "space junk," in orbit around Earth. Some space junk eventually falls to Earth. Some of it burns up in Earth's atmosphere. Some of the space junk in Earth's upper atmosphere could continue to orbit the planet indefinitely.

Even very tiny pieces of space junk can cause problems. People are working to solve these problems. Organizations that send satellites into space can design their spacecraft to make less waste. They can track larger space junk so that spacecraft can avoid crashes. They can even retrieve larger pieces of the space junk, but this is expensive. Some researchers suggest using lasers to push pieces of space junk out of the way of spacecraft.

Discuss ideas for solving the space junk problem with your group. How can people prevent the creation of more space junk? Record ideas from your discussion below.

Check Your Understanding

1 Which of the following human activities have a positive impact on the environment? Select each correct answer.

A ◯ recycling

B ◯ deforestation

C ◯ conservation

D ◯ reducing waste

E ◯ land development

2 Which of the following statements **best** describes how farming can have a negative impact on the environment?

A ◯ Contour plowing is used to prevent soil erosion.

B ◯ Pesticides run off into streams and rivers.

C ◯ Aluminum cans and bottles are recycled.

D ◯ Land developers clear land for housing.

3 Sort each of the following activities into the correct group. Record the activities from the list in the correct boxes.

| Factory pollution | Habitat loss | Terracing |
| Recycling | Burning fossil fuels | Wind turbine power |

Positive Impact	Negative Impact

4 What positive effects does recycling, reducing, and reusing products have on Earth's resources? Record your ideas below.

_____

_____

_____

_____

5 Study the diagram below. How does this diagram illustrate how pollutants can build up in water?

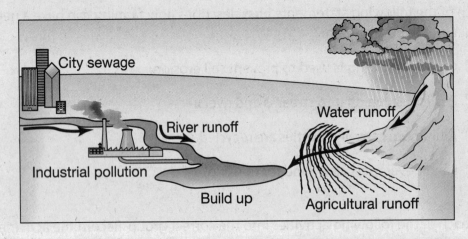

_____

_____

_____

_____

Engineering

Engineers are problem solvers. They solve real-world problems by designing something new—something that people need or want.

What kinds of problems do engineers solve? Some of the problems are very complex. How do you build a tunnel under a river to take thousands of commuters to work each day? Some of the problems are simpler. How do you design a vest so that people can run safely in the dark? In this unit, you will learn more about the engineer's design process. You will even solve a few problems yourself.

Lesson 15

Defining a Problem

Look at the photos above.

What do you see in the photos? What is happening in the photos? Discuss the photos with your group. Record your observations below.

What problems could the people in the photos face? How are the problems similar? How are they different?

Look at the photo above. Discuss the photo with your group.

What do you see in the photo? What is happening in the photo?

The swimmer has solved one problem of swimming underwater. He is wearing goggles to protect his eyes and to be able to see underwater. But what problem must be solved in order for him to swim underwater for a long period of time?

Look Ahead

A problem is something that needs to be addressed or solved. A solution is a way to solve a problem. But what is an engineering problem? You will learn about engineering problems and solutions in this lesson.

Explore!

Eggs in a Nest

Materials

- Plastic Easter basket grass
- Paper
- Cardboard
- Plastic egg
- String

Steps

1 Describe the egg and the nest that your teacher shows you.

_____

_____

2 The egg needs to be in the nest. However, the egg cannot come into direct contact with human hands. Describe the problem.

_____

_____

3 With your group, determine solutions for how to get the egg into the nest without harming the egg. How does each solution meet the requirement of placing the egg safely in the nest without touching it with your hands?

_____

_____

_____

4 Now consider solutions for getting the egg into the nest by using one of these materials: paper, string, or cardboard. You may handle the paper, string, and cardboard to help you come up with solutions. Each possible solution should use only one of the materials. Use the space below to describe your solutions.

_____

_____

_____

_____

5 Present your group's solutions to the class. Compare your ideas with other groups.

Think About It

What are the features of a possible solution when using only paper, string, or cardboard?

What are the limits of each solution? How might you decide on the best solution?

Understand

You solve problems every day. What makes an everyday problem different from an engineering problem? An engineering problem is one that can be solved with a new or improved design. The design can be for an object, tool, process, or system. The first step is to define the engineering problem. To define any problem, the following three questions must be answered:

What is the need?
Who has the problem?
Why is it important to solve?

Using these three questions, you can write a problem statement. A problem statement is a clear one-sentence description of the problem. Think about the photo of the runner at night on the first page of this lesson. The runner has a need to be seen by drivers at night. So, in this case, the runner has the problem. It is important for the runner to be seen so that he is not hit by a car. So, the problem statement is:

A runner needs to be seen at night so that the runner is not hit by a car.

Whether an engineering problem is big or small, the steps to solving it are always the same. An engineer's basic approach to problem solving is the design process. The first step of this process is defining the problem using the questions above to produce the problem statement.

Think about the underwater swimmer from earlier in the lesson. What if the swimmer wants or needs to swim underwater for a long period of time? Define this problem by answering the three questions above. Then write a problem statement for the swimmer.

In the next step of the design process, an engineer uses science to solve the problem. Look at the photo below on the left. The photo shows a man using scuba equipment. The equipment was designed so that a person can breathe and swim underwater for long periods of time.

Would the design and use of scuba equipment be a solution to the problem statement you wrote for the swimmer? Explain your answer.

Look at the photo above on the right. The photo shows a reflective vest. The vest was designed with a certain feature so that it could be seen at night.

Would the design and use of the reflective vest be a solution to the problem statement for the runner at night? Explain your answer.

Think back to the Explore activity, in which you had to find ways to place an egg in a nest without using your hands. A successful solution must have the desired feature of the egg not coming into direct contact with human hands. Engineers often determine the desired features of a possible solution to a problem. This method allows them to produce a successful solution.

A desired feature of a successful solution is called a criterion. The plural form of the word *criterion* is *criteria*. In a successful solution, the design meets all the criteria.

Look back to the photo of the man wearing scuba equipment. What would have been some of the criteria in designing this equipment? Explain.

The possible solutions to any engineering problem are limited by available materials or resources. Again, think about the Explore activity with the egg and the nest. You could probably think of many different solutions for placing an egg in its nest without the egg coming into direct human contact. However, when you were limited to using only paper, string, or cardboard, your solutions were also limited.

Limitations of possible solutions are called constraints. Limitations might be placed on materials, time, or costs. Think about the design of scuba equipment. The equipment allows a person to swim underwater for long periods of time. The person must be able to wear or transport the equipment when they are moving underwater.

Think about the design of the scuba equipment. What would have been some of the constraints in designing this equipment? Explain.

Go Further

Suppose you have thought of a possible solution to an engineering problem. You have also identified the criteria and the constraints. How could you best present your solution, along with its criteria and constraints? The next step is to write a proposal.

A proposal is often a written plan that is evaluated by a group of people. A proposal can present a solution to a problem statement. A proposal must be clear, or easy to understand, because the writer of the proposal is often not the person who constructs the solution.

A proposal needs to meet the specified criteria and account for any constraints. Proposals should have solutions that are safe to build or use. In addition, proposals should have solutions that can be done by the due dates, or deadlines.

Here is another problem to consider. In this problem, a growing city needs a way for vehicles to cross to the other side of a river. One proposal is to build a bridge for vehicles to cross over the river. Another proposal is to build a tunnel for vehicles to cross under the river. Look at the photos below, which show a bridge and a tunnel.

Look at the two solution proposals below. Consider the criteria, or features, of each proposed solution. Then consider the constraints, or limitations, of each proposed solution. The features and constraints determine the advantages and disadvantages of each design.

Proposal: Build a Bridge	Proposal: Build a Tunnel

Time it takes to build: 4 years
Cost: $110 million
Possible vehicle volume per day: 50,000
 	
Advantages:
    Less expensive than a tunnel
    Does not require lighting 24 hours a day
    Requires less security than a tunnel
 	
Disadvantages:
    Allows passage of fewer vehicles each day than a bridge
    Does not allow tall ships to pass through the waterway
    Can be closed due to weather
	Time it takes to build: 4 years
	Cost: $250 million
	Possible vehicle volume per day: 75,000
	
	Advantages:
	    Allows passage of more vehicles each day than a bridge
	    Allows tall ships to pass through the waterway
	
	Disadvantages:
	    More expensive than a bridge
	    Requires lighting 24 hours a day
	    Requires more security than a bridge
	    Can be closed due to flooding

Based on the two proposals, would you approve a tunnel or a bridge? Explain your answer.

Suppose you had five years but only $200 million to build a tunnel or a bridge. Which proposal would you approve? Explain your answer.

Engineers work to find solutions to many human needs and concerns. The photo below shows food that has been thrown away as garbage. Did you know that one-third to one-half of the world's food is wasted or thrown away each year? Engineers are working to find ways to reduce food waste.

Imagine that you are working as a food engineer. Write a problem statement that deals with food waste.

List some ideas for a proposal that has a solution to your food waste problem statement.

1   In engineering design, which of the following can be constraints? Select all that apply.

A ○ review of several design proposals

B ○ amount of materials available

C ○ design of a successful solution

D ○ limitation on cost

E ○ early deadline

2   To be approved, the design for a new car had to have certain criteria. Select the **best** word to describe criteria.

A ○ losses

B ○ features

C ○ damages

D ○ categories

3   Which statement about a solution proposal to an engineering problem is **not** correct?

A ○ The proposal should provide a plan that meets a due date.

B ○ The proposal should be clear and easy to understand.

C ○ The proposal should not consider safety factors.

D ○ The proposal should meet specified criteria.

4 Mark with an X to show whether each item below is a constraint or a criterion for building a house.

	Criterion	Constraint
The house should have large rooms.		
The house should cost no more than $100,000.		
The house should take no more than two years to build.		

5 Write a problem statement that addresses getting your books and school supplies home after school.

_____

_____

_____

_____

6 Imagine that you are a spaceflight engineer. What problems need to be solved in order for a person to travel into space?

_____

_____

_____

_____

_____

Lesson 16

Designing, Testing, and Revising a Solution

Look at the photo above.

Discuss the photo with a partner. Describe the trunk. Do you think there is something inside? Why? What do you think might be inside the trunk? Record your ideas below.

Suppose the key that opens the trunk is lost. The owner of the trunk does not remember what he put in it before it was locked. He wants to know what is inside the trunk, but he does not want to damage or destroy the trunk in order to find out. What problem does the owner of the trunk face in this situation?

How can the owner determine the contents of the trunk? With your partner, brainstorm a list of ways in which the owner could determine what is inside the trunk. The solutions cannot include destroying or damaging the trunk. List any pros or cons for each solution. A *pro* is an advantage, or something that is favorable. A *con* is a disadvantage, or something that is unfavorable. Record your ideas in the table below.

Solution	Pros	Cons

What limitations does the owner face in finding a solution to this problem?

Look Ahead

You probably thought of many solutions to determining the contents of the trunk. What do you have to consider when you come up with solutions? How can solutions be tested? You will explore these questions in this lesson.

Mysterious Mixtures

Materials

- Mixture of two substances
- Funnel
- Water
- Mixing spoon
- Pan
- Coffee filter
- Plastic container

Steps

1 Observe the mixture. What do you think the mixture is made up of?

_____

2 Suppose that the parts of the mixture need to be separated. You can use only the materials you have. What is the problem? Record your problem statement.

_____

_____

3 Use the Internet and resource books to research your problem. Describe each of your solutions below. Evaluate each solution to determine what criteria, or requirements, of the problem the solution satisfies. List any pros or cons.

Solution	Criteria	Pros	Cons

4 As a group, pick the best solution. This is the solution that you will test. Discuss with your group the necessary steps to test this solution. Record the steps below.

_____

_____

_____

_____

_____

5 Follow the steps to test your solution. Record your observations below.

_____

_____

Think About It

Were there any steps that did not work as you had expected? What effect did this have on your solution?

Share your solution and observations with other groups, and listen to their solutions and observations. With your group, discuss the different solutions that other groups came up with. Which solutions worked best? Explain.

Understand

Technological design is the process of using science to design new technology to solve problems. To design something means to make a plan for it. A solution is a way of solving a problem.

The first step in the design process is to identify a problem you want to solve.

Think back to the Explore activity. What was the problem you faced in the activity?

Look at the photo below. A student walks his dog every day. But the student also needs to walk his dog in the evening after dinner. In winter it can be dark. The student states his problem: "I need to be sure that people driving cars will see my dog in the dark." Then he can do research to find out what is already known about this problem.

Designing a solution to your problem is the next step in the process. Research about the problem should be done before designing your solution. There are many ways to research the problem. You can use the Internet to find out more about the problem. You can use reference books like textbooks. You can even talk to an expert.

Sometimes it might even be helpful to research a similar problem to yours. That way you can see what has been tried, what has worked, and what has not worked. This information can then be applied to your problem. The solution may not relate exactly, but it can give you a good idea of where to start with your solution.

What research did you do in the Explore activity? How did it help you to come up with solutions to the problem of separating the mixture?

Part of the design process is identifying any criteria, or requirements, for the solution. For the student who needs to walk his dog after dinner, the requirement is that the dog needs to be seen when it is dark outside. Problems can have more than one requirement. What if the student wants the solution to include a way to identify his dog as well? This would be an additional requirement for the solution.

Requirements often include price, availability, and ease of use. For example, the solution to the dog walker's problem should be something that is easy to use. If the solution is too difficult to use, then it may not be helpful to the dog walker.

In the Explore activity, what requirement for separating the materials did you have to satisfy? Was price a factor? What about time needed and the ease of separating the mixture?

There are many ways for a problem to be solved. It is best to list all solutions that you can think of. After you have your list of possible solutions, you can compare them to your criteria. One solution for walking a dog when it is dark may be a reflective vest that the dog can wear. Another solution may be a flashing collar. Look at the picture below.

Reflective vest

Flashing collar

Which solution seems to best meet all the requirements, or criteria?

By trying out both solutions, the student could find out which one is better. The better solution should satisfy all the requirements, or criteria.

Once you have a solution, you need to test it to see how well it works. This is the next step in the design process. It is usually done in different conditions. For the student who needs to walk his dog when it is dark, the solution might need to be tested under different weather conditions. Will the reflective vest hold up in the rain or snow?

Performing tests on your solution provides helpful information. The result from a test can help you to identify the parts of your solution that do not work. Based on this information, you can then modify your solution so that it works better.

How could you improve the method you used to separate the mixture of two substances in the Explore activity? Work with a partner to come up with ideas.

Sharing your solution is an important part of the design process. This is also the final step in the process. There are different ways to share your solution. You could share your solution by talking about it in a group or as a class. You could share what you learned by writing a paper, making a poster, or even building a model.

In the photo above on the left, engineers are sharing their designs with their colleagues. Scientists share their solutions in this way. They may present their work in front of a large group at a conference, as shown in the photo above on the right. At conferences, scientists can talk to other scientists about their solutions. They receive feedback from the other scientists. This allows them to reflect on their solutions and make changes.

How did you communicate your solution? How did talking with others and seeing their solutions affect your design?

Go Further

Oil spills in the ocean are a big problem. When oil spills into the ocean, animal and plant life near the spill can be destroyed or endangered. Oil spills can happen when people are not careful with the design and control of ships that are carrying oil. Spills can also happen when people intentionally spill oil into the ocean. Look at the photo below of a turtle that has been covered in oil from an ocean spill.

How might scientists test their ideas when designing a solution to an oil spill?

What factors do scientists need to take into consideration when designing a solution to this problem?

Oil spills can also cause oil to wash up on beaches and shorelines, as shown in the photos below. The beaches and shorelines need to be closed to the public until they can be cleaned.

Suppose you are one of the scientists who have been asked to find a solution to a recent oil spill that is washing oil up on beaches and shoreline areas. Work with your group to design a possible solution to this problem.

Solution	
Criteria that the solution satisfies	
Pros	
Cons	

1   Which of the following are important steps in the design process? Select all that apply.

   A ☐ Identify any criteria, or requirements, for the solution.

   B ☐ Design your solution first, and then research the problem.

   C ☐ Share your solution by discussing it with others.

   D ☐ Test your solution under only one condition.

   E ☐ Identify a problem you want to solve.

   F ☐ Design a solution.

2   Suppose your dog has fallen into a deep hole in your backyard. The dog is not able to get out on its own. Identify which criteria should be applied to the solution for getting your dog out of the hole. Mark an X in the box that tells whether each statement is or is not a criterion.

	Criterion	Not a Criterion
You cannot go into the hole.		
The animal should not be injured in the rescue.		
Time—you should rescue the animal as quickly as possible.		
You can go to the store to buy whatever you need.		

3   You like to do your homework near an open window. Sometimes your papers blow
    around in the breeze. Identify the problem and then list a possible solution.

    _____

    _____

    _____

    _____

4   Is there ever only one way to approach, or solve, a problem? Explain your answer.

    _____

    _____

    _____

    _____

5   Why is it important to test your design solution?

    _____

    _____

    _____

    _____

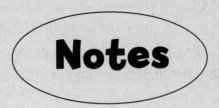

Notes

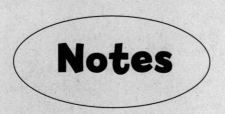

Notes

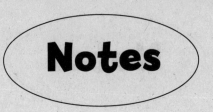
Notes